Celery Day

Steve Queen

Copyright © 2014 Steve Queen

All rights reserved.

ISBN: 1505516188
ISBN-13: 978-1505516180

Celery Day

DEDICATION

This book is dedicated to my family, who live out the truths woven through these pages every day. It was during one of our family meals that the core concept behind "Celery Day" was sparked.

ACKNOWLEDGMENTS

I thank my family and friends who reviewed the manuscript early on and provided candid feedback. My earthly journey is deeply enriched by our relationship.

Table of Contents

Chapter 1: You Can't Be Serious 1

Chapter 2: First Trip In The New Era 4

Chapter 3: What To Do? 8

Chapter 4: Kate..14

Chapter 5: Three Weeks To Be There 19

Chapter 6: Discovery 22

Chapter 7: Time To Do It...32

Chapter 8: Transition 39

Chapter 9: Kids 42

Chapter 10: He Got It...45

Chapter 11: The Familiar 53

Chapter 12: Owning It To The Root 62

Chapter 13: Never Thought I Would Miss It..............70

Chapter 14: Library Talk..75

Chapter 15: Connection 82

Chapter 1: You Can't Be Serious

I got up from the dinner table and wandered into the living room. I wasn't quite sure what I thought about what Brian had said. An organic farm? Really? I mean why would we do an organic farm? I just couldn't understand right then how that would make any sense. I had a successful career. I earned a good salary. The company where I had worked for the last 23 years had sold and I came out well. Why on earth would I - at almost 50 years old - want to have anything to do with working on a farm or trying to run a farm and putting my own money at risk? None of it made any sense to me.

On the other hand for Brian - having just graduated from college less than a year ago - and being, well, Brian my extremely green, extremely globally-conscious, semi-hippie son who I seem to have understood less and less over the last four years -   for him running and owning an organic farm is just the best thing he could ever think about doing. This is the kid who my wife and I raised, who began saying three or four years ago that he not only wanted to make a living, he wanted to make a difference. And, if he could make a difference while he made a living that would be the best thing ever. So he got a degree that was about as far from engineering and business as you could ever imagine. With his liberal arts degree I wasn't sure what he was going to be or do… maybe teach? I don't know. Don't get me wrong, I try to be open-minded about all this but I just couldn't see where Brian was headed.

Well, at dinner we had spoken about the fact that the farm was now mine. My dad had passed away just a week earlier and Mom had passed on a few months before. In the will the farm was left to me. My initial thought was, "Well, more than likely we will sell it and use part of that money as seed money to maybe help Brian get off the ground with whatever it is he wants to do. If he wants to have a coffee shop or restaurant or some sort of concert-poetry venue thing, wonderful. At least he would have a good financial start." I'm not trying to be tacky, I'm just saying I've continued to struggle with whether he has his feet on the ground at all about how business really works. Honestly, I think sometimes that my wife and I - without meaning to - just spoiled him. When he worked a few jobs through college they never lasted long. I just wasn't sure he had the first clue about what he was suggesting.

"Okay, so now what do we do with the farm?" asked Kate. I recommended selling it. I asked Brian what he thought. He fidgeted with the peas on his plate for a little bit and then smiled and said, "Think about it, Dad." He looked at his mom, "Organic farming is huge and it's getting bigger. People are willing to pay more money for better food. I mean, just look at our own family. Mom started buying organic a couple of years ago. We are paying more for groceries than we ever have and we're getting better stuff. Think of how many people here in Oklahoma City we know who do the same thing. Think about the people we know in Tulsa doing the same thing, and others all over the state and the nation. Organic farming has just exploded because people are actually willing to make it work in the marketplace. They're willing to spend the money to get good quality food and to support the farmers."

I just stared at him in absolute disbelief. I said, "Wait a minute. Are you seriously suggesting that I leave my company and we go become farmers?" He smiled and said, "Yeah, that's exactly what I'm suggesting; that we can do it and we should do it." Of course, I looked across the table at my wife and I said, "Do you want to be a farmer's wife, a farmer yourself? And do you really think it would be worth moving away from OKC to go live on my parents' farm?" She looked at Brian and back at me and said, "You know, honestly, Mike, I never really thought about it but I think we should be open to this. This could be the best thing ever for us. I mean, really, think about the conversations you and I have had now for quite some time. You've had a great career. You've worked very hard. You've done some very challenging things. You traveled. You worked long hours. You paid the price." Then, she glanced over at Brian and said, "He paid a price for you, too, so you can have the life that you've had so far." He stared at his plate and said, "I know that." Then he looked at me with a look that I was hoping I would see one day and he said, "I want you to know I get it. I appreciate what you've done and how hard you've worked Dad. I realize we all have to choose our path and you chose yours. I have matured. I have listened and I realize money doesn't just pop up out of the ground. And, I appreciate what you've done like Mom is saying. But, I've overheard you and Mom talk from time to time about maybe changing careers. I see it in your face. You really do look ready for something different."

Well, at that point I took a deep breath and said, "You know, clearly I need to think about this. I need to really weigh this out; we all do, because this is a huge, huge decision for us. Thankfully the farm has been willed to me so we don't have to buy it. But, this farm can't take all our money to run it. I guess it's worth thinking about. Let's mull it over and go out to the farm and take a look. We need to go out there anyway to go through Mom and Dad's personal effects next week. So, when we go there to do that we will just take a hard look at it as a business, right?" They both nodded their heads and said, "Yeah that sounds good." I said, "Well in that case, let's put all this on the shelf for now, have dessert and enjoy some time together."

Chapter 2: First Trip In The New Era

Brian, Kate and I made the drive to my parents' farm, which had so recently become my farm, our farm. It was a nice drive through some beautiful country and only took about an hour and a half. I noticed how fresh the air smelled after we got just 10 or 15 miles outside the metro OKC area. The closer we got to the farm, the more my childhood memories returned. Most were good; some were not so good. My dad had grown up on the farm and moved to his own house when he turned 18 and married my mom. He continued to work the farm with his dad, his mom and some hired hands. It was a hard way to make a living, but they made it work. When grandpa passed away unexpectedly at age 56, grandma asked if my folks wanted to move into the farm house to save some money. She didn't mind that they would keep the house from being so quiet all the time either. They agreed and moved into the house. They lived there from then on.

I grew up in that house and working on the farm myself. I knew when I turned 14 that I did not want to be a career farmer like my dad. I didn't tell him that until I was 16. He just got really quiet when I told him. He said time would tell whether I really wanted to walk away from a family business that was well established or not. I did. When I turned 18 I left for college and never once considered being a farmer. Engineering and business were what interested me. I did not mind the idea of working mostly in an air conditioned, dry, clean office either. Dad never understood how I could do that. It seemed so confining and narrow and foreign to him. I felt the same way about the farm, at least the "confining and narrow" parts. The farm was not foreign to me early in my career, but it had become more foreign as time passed.

We turned down the last gravel road that took us south, and led to the farm. The same mailbox was there that Dad and I had installed 30 years earlier. It was welded to an old chain whose links had been welded together, so it was a bit of a visual surprise to people the first time they saw it. It looked like it should fall down, because chains don't stand upright on their own. Dad was always doing different things that made people stop and think. He thought that kept life more on the interesting side than just always doing what "everyone else does" or "what is expected". That may seem odd for a farmer, but that was Dad, always willing to look at new things, or look at old things from a different angle.

We pulled into the driveway and sat for a minute. We had visited Dad a month earlier. Prior to that it had been 5 or 6 months since we had been out. I know, it seems unthinkable now to be an hour and a half away and let that kind of time pass without visiting. But, isn't that how it always seems once someone passes on?

I turned the engine off and said, "Well, let's go inside and see what's in there. I think just getting started is important." We all got out of the car and walked up the steps to the porch. I found the key to the door and turned the lock cylinder, heard the "click" of the bolt sliding into place inside the door, and I just stood there. This would be the first time for me to enter the house without one or more of my parents being there. I wasn't sure how that would hit me. So, I took a deep breath and opened the door.

That old, familiar… not very foreign… smell filled my nose and my mind with history. I remembered meals, holidays, vigorous discussions, laughter, tears and biscuits… lots of biscuits. Mom always made the best biscuits I had ever eaten. Like most families we knew, a lot of our interaction happened around the table, and the table usually included a basket of Mom's biscuits. She wanted to nurture our family in every way, which she did. She taught us all -

Dad, me and various cousins, aunts, uncles and others who were frequently working and eating with us - the value of embracing every moment of our day as a gift from God and making it count. She said there were no small acts born of love, only great ones - no matter who sees it. Dad challenged Mom and me - and anyone else around - to look beyond the surface of things, to see the story, the dance, the battle and the humor of life. My parents both affected me deeply and shaped who I became. As I stood in the entry way remembering these things I smiled. Mom and Dad had both run their race, trained me the best they knew how and now their legacy continued to ripple through me. It was both a sober and encouraging moment for me; one of those moments where the big story of life is clear and present.

The kitchen looked the same as it had for 15 years. The same appliances and jars and towels were in the same places they had always been. I thought how my mom would never again adjust the towels so they hung straight down at 90 degrees to the floor. Dad would never again open the jar full of cashews to get a snack before tackling another project. The feelings hit me pretty hard. I teared up and had to sit down at the kitchen table. I cried. Kate and Brian cried. We all sat there thinking, feeling, knowing we missed Mom and Dad immensely.

After five minutes or so we dried our eyes, had a good hug and decided to get on with the task at hand. Since we weren't sure what we would do with the farm, we didn't want to have an estate sale and sell off everything. We decide instead to look for very personal items that we knew we wanted to keep. We identified a mixer in the kitchen, the table Dad had made that stood in between Mom and Dad's chairs and the family clock that great granddad had brought over from Switzerland when he emigrated to America. There was Dad's old straight razor, the first and only quilt Mom had made when she was a teenager, Dad's shotgun and several other things that had some sentimental value to one or more of us. As we looked in the master bedroom closet, through the clothes and the shoes, Brian noticed a box, or chest, in the back corner. He brought it out. It was made of wood with strips of metal attached to it. It was sturdy and rustic, but also beautiful. It had a locking hasp. When we tried to open it, we couldn't because it was locked. We knew there had to be a key somewhere, and so began a lengthy search. We looked in every drawer in the bedroom and in the study to no avail. Kate eventually remembered seeing a key in the pantry, hanging on a hook. I got the key and gave it to her. It worked. This was classic Dad. If someone really wanted to steal the box and break it open they could. But, Dad wasn't going to make it easy. He wanted anyone who would do something like that to have to stop and think about what they were doing. He no doubt thought that might even make them leave the chest alone out of a sudden sense of respect for what might be in there. I don't know about that, but I do know that I was ready to see what was so important that Dad kept it under lock and key.

We didn't find important documents regarding land ownership, stocks, bonds and the like. Anything like that was kept in a fireproof box or in a bank safe deposit box. The things in this chest were of a different kind of value. There were things that mattered to Dad from his own life, his journey on this earth. He had saved various artifacts from interactions with friends and some traveling he had done. I knew some of the stories behind the objects, but not all. He had left a journal in the chest, which I looked forward to reading at some point. As we got to the bottom of the chest we found two things that were unexpected, yet connected. At the time I had no idea how connected they were.

Chapter 3: What To Do?

We closed the chest and put it back in its place. I made some coffee with that clear, clean well water drawn from deep in the earth. We sat down in the living room to discuss more about what to do with the farm.

Kate said, "Option 1 is to sell the farm. Option 2 is to try to lease the farm. Option 3 is to run the farm." She has always been good at bringing clarity to issues and keeping conversations rooted in what is to be done. I chimed in, "Okay, if we sell the farm we would probably sell to one of the big corporations who want to expand into this area. They would get 640 acres of prime, river bottom farmland that has grown cotton, corn, oats, blackberries, peaches and a few other crops in more recent years. We would get a big stack of money. What we would lose is the opportunity to ever visit this place, to come here and relax or possibly to work this land." Brian said, "Dad, I know you own the place now, but since we are talking about it, right here and now, it grieves me to think of giving up this land, our history, the potential that is here… and maybe the idea that we really could make this a thriving organic farm." In that moment I saw a spark in Brian's eyes. He looked like he was really serious about this place, about the idea that this land could be a meaningful part of his future, our future. I looked at Kate. She said, "If we sell it, we get more money. We sell not only the earth, the water and the house, we sell all the future potential for us that is here." None of us were willing to move forward with selling, at least not yet.

"Option 2, we can own it and lease it to someone else to work," said Kate. She continued, "That way, we can still visit if we just want to get out in the country for awhile. We would make money each year as long as someone leased the land." Brian and I nodded our heads. Leasing would allow me to keep working at my job. I didn't know what

Brian would do. Maybe he could hire on to work on the farm as an employee of the lessee? That way he could see if farming was all he thought it might be. He could live either in the house or close by, which would help him develop some real-world independence. It seemed leasing might be the best and most reasonable option.

"Option 3," said Brian, "is that we work this farm together and help make a difference while we make a living. Mom, Dad… think how cool it would be to see the work we did every day right in front of us! We are about an hour from Tulsa and about an hour and a half from OKC. They both have plenty of people who are - today - buying more and more organic produce. And, they prefer to get it from as nearby as possible. Think of the restaurants, especially the farm-to-table places who would love to have more options for their patrons! Think about right around here in McAlester and Muskogee with the bed and breakfast owners. Ft. Smith is less than 2 hours away. There are plenty of people within reasonable driving distance who would buy our produce if we grow it sustainably. I know we can do it! I've been thinking about this a lot and I would be totally wiling to commit to it, to move here and work really hard to see this happen." Kate and I looked at each other. The clear nonverbal message we exchanged was, "Well, he sounds more serious and more focused than I've seen him in a very long time. I think he really would do this. What about us? Would we?" I said, "I tell you what," and looked at both Brian and Kate, "I am willing to seriously consider moving here and owning and operating this as an organic farm. I'm going to do my homework as usual, think, talk with you and pray about this. This is a big, big deal. A week ago I would not have given it a second thought, but that time is past. I don't want to miss what could be something wonderful, even if it seems a bit crazy right now. Would you both agree to make this something you think, pray and work through just as seriously?" They both said, "Yes, absolutely." We finished the coffee and decided we needed to head to Krebs for some great Italian food for lunch. I had not been there in over ten years, but it was just as good as ever. We drove back to OKC in almost complete silence, with a lot rolling around inside our heads and hearts.

With about a half hour left to drive, Kate asked, "So, what are you guys thinking about regarding the farm and what to do? Why don't we talk about it now while it's fresh? Obviously we aren't going to decide anything right now, but we've always been candid with each other and I'd like to know what you are thinking and feeling."

Brian said, "Okay, I'll go first. Like a lot of my friends I've dabbled in a lot of things: hobbies, jobs, majors in school, theater, a few bands I played in and on and on. I think that's normal for humans to experiment and find their way.

While I respect Dad, I don't want to do what he does for a living - not even close. He gets a lot out of his work. I realize I have benefitted from all his work. But, I decided a few years ago that I want to do what feeds my soul, what I feel strongly about to make a difference in the world and earn my living in the process. I fully understand that I may be in for a rude awakening as to what my standard of living may be, but I at least want to try it. I won't live off gifts from you guys - that's just parasitic and it keeps people immature. You both want me to make my own way in the world and I want the same thing.

I've realized that I just don't have the musical talent to make it in a band, not really. I've always received good reviews of my poetry and other writing from teachers and friends. I actually sold a few copies of a small book of poems at an arts fair last year. However, that is not a way to make a living. So, I have been thinking through options for making a difference and making a living in the process. When Dad told us he had inherited the farm, I instantly began to wonder what possibilities that could bring to my life. My friends and I have been eating at some great restaurants in Midtown and Uptown OKC and in Tulsa on Cherry Street for years. More and more of the restaurants make a point to say their food is sourced as locally and organically as possible. I love that! It excites me to think that people are providing something as essential and basic to life as food, while being responsible citizens of the planet… and they earn a living at it! Now, I have the opportunity to not only be happy for them doing that, but I can do that too! It would mean moving away from OKC and not just 20 minutes away, an hour and a half away. That's a real social price I would have to pay to work the organic farm.

I think now as an adult I'm feeling more and more what Dad calls "the double edged sword of opportunity" - excitement for what can be and fear of losing what you have today. For me, I have to get alone and meditate and pray over big decisions like this. I don't just want to put some facts on one side of the "mental scale" and other facts on the other side and see which way it tilts. Facts are facts, but it's the heart, passion, commitment and the prospect of a better future that keep us going, right? I mean whether you are an engineer, accountant, philosopher or painter, isn't that still what keeps you going? There has to be more than a paycheck that gets me out of bed. I want to sink my feet and hands and heart and soul into something I believe in down to my toenails."

Kate said, "Okay, I'll go next. You know, my grandparents had a farm when I was growing up. In the summers my brother and sister and I would go stay with our grandparents for a few weeks. It was work but it was fun being on the farm. However, as kids we weren't trying to make a living at it either. I know that we really don't have to make a living from the farm, but honestly, I don't want it to become a 12 or 14 hour a day hobby. I surely don't want us to take it easy and hire people to do all the work. I also don't want the money we have been blessed with to be poured out on some crazy idea that fails. I want that money to be invested in ways that help people.

As far as daily life on the farm, I can imagine some aspects of it. It would be more quiet than OKC. There would be no more neighborhood walks where we spoke to half a dozen families as we walked. On the farm, neighbors are a car ride - or truck ride - away. I might actually go get eggs from the hens directly instead of a store. By the way, where is the closest store to the farm? Would a trip to the store be a monthly event? Would we spend many hours together every day talking about the work we are doing, the beauty of God's creation and being thankful for the life we have? Would we spend many hours together every day wondering why we got ourselves into this never ending circle of trying and failing and being exhausted, especially with Dad and me in our mid- forties?

I know this, Mike: you have said you are still happy in your career - and I think you are for the most part. But, ever since the company was purchased, things have not been the same for you. You still do great work. The team still makes things other companies buy. All the parts continue to move and generate what they need to generate. But, I know you. I hear you sigh more than you used to. I see you stare off into space more than you used to. You seems a little restless, like you are searching.

I've known for some time that a big change is coming. I think you know it too, but you tend to focus on the task at hand so much that you don't talk often about the distant future. I think Brian clearly feels he needs direction, even immersion, in something meaningful to him. We have a big decision in front of us. I know where I lean right now, but I need to weigh this out some more to be absolutely sure." I said, "Well, I'll go last. For me, the decision about what to do with the farm would actually be easier if we didn't have options. If I had just lost my job, moving and operating the farm would seem like a viable career change. Or, if we had huge medical bills or massive loans we couldn't pay, selling the farm to pay off those bills would seem like a straightforward choice. So, we have the pleasure and the pain of options. I've loved my career in the energy field and I still do. But, I have thought recently that if I were ever going to change careers, now would probably be a good time to do it. I just couldn't think of what my next career would be.

I thought about being a consultant in the oil and gas industry, or maybe even a guest lecturer in college classes. I can say that the farm never crossed my mind. In my industry, I'm used to being one of the most qualified people in the room. On the farm, I think I would feel very under qualified. I could learn how to farm from books and online resources. But, most of all, I would have to learn by getting in the dirt, watching the folks who work the land and letting them be my teachers and trainers. That sounds exciting, but also scary to be honest. I don't want to jump into something and then realize I can't do it or don't want to do it. Frankly, I don't have a strong inclination one way or another right now. I just want to keep an open mind."

Chapter 4: Kate

A few days after returning to OKC I started thinking about the research I knew I would need to do to make a decision I felt confident in. Kate would be more intuitive about the decision, but she would research some key specifics. Brian would just want to immerse himself in something that could be truly awesome. I've seen him work very hard at things he believed in and wanted. Frankly I had not seen that since he graduated college. I wanted him not to feel adrift any longer. But, I could not imagine me leaving my career, my executive income and industry acumen behind just to dig in the dirt with Brian because it would make him smile… for awhile. I mean, I love Brian and I do want him happy, but what if this whole organic farm thing is just a whim? What if it's the coolest thing ever for about six months and then he wants to move away and do something else? Would Kate and I keep farming? And what about Kate? I knew that if she said yes to farming, it would take some kind of catastrophic failure to get her to quit.

Kate was never a quitter. From the time I met her in high school I was struck by her way, her confidence and humility. She made people feel welcome around her. She cared about her friends and it showed in her words and actions. As I got to know her better, I learned that her family owned a dry cleaning business. Kate had grown up in the business, working long hours in tough conditions since she was a child. She learned the value of work, not only to earn money but to show you care about people through your work. She wanted people to pick up clean, crisp, sharp looking clothes from her family's shop. She liked to work the cash register sometimes so she could see customers' faces when they received their garments.

She learned from her family's business that the work isn't over until it's over. The notion of working an 8 hour day and going home was foreign to her parents. They would stop work for dinner in the evening and almost always work another hour or two or three before going home. Kate learned that if you want to succeed you have to count the cost of the endeavor, commit and stick with it. She did just that when she assessed her options for college. She kept working at the family dry cleaning shop through college when she could have had an easier job and more free time with college friends. Why did she do it? She cared for her parents and siblings who worked there. She didn't want to let them down, and she needed a job anyway. To her, work was always about more than money.

My relationship with Kate grew during college. In hindsight, she was evaluating me and what it would be like to be married to me the whole time. Sure, we both had that spark of romantic love from the beginning. We enjoyed each others' company, we laughed, we went out on dates, we danced, we stayed up late talking and stared up at the stars often. All the while, she was checking in her own heart to see if I was the right one for her, long term. She was evaluating in her head what the challenges would be, marrying an engineer… even if I was the only engineer she knew who also wrote her poems.

When I did ask her to marry me, she already knew her answer. We were married just a few weeks after graduating college. We knew we wanted to have a child soon, which led us to decide that it was time for Kate to leave her family's dry cleaning shop. She was going to launch into a new career that was intimately tied to my new career. She knew it wouldn't be easy, and that was okay. She loved me, she already loved our child who was on the way and she was no stranger to hard work for the people she loved.

Kate became the Office Manager for our brand new engineering company. It was started by Kate, me and three other recent college engineering graduates with big ideas for getting oil and gas out of the ground - and even some ideas about harvesting alternative energy - but no idea how to run a business. One of the three was Danielle, whose dad had started a similar company 20 years earlier in her home state. He had done well and offered us fresh graduates the seed money to start our company, for 20% ownership in the company. We took him up on the offer. We did very well, thanks in part to his advice at some critical junctures. We patented several devices that became widely used in the oil and gas industry. We developed devices for alternative energy as well including wind and solar power. Early on we did well enough to buy out Danielle's dad and he made a nice profit.

In the early years of the business, Kate or I would take Brian to the office with us. Very early on Kate had the idea of having an in-office daycare for our staff. She screened applicants to work the daycare and set up the procedures for everything from access to the daycare room, to cleanliness, etc. In just a few years the daycare expanded to three rooms to accommodate the various ages of our team's children. The onsite daycare was just another example of Kate's deeply felt and down-to-earth love for people.

Over the years we hired more engineers and plenty of office staff and field representatives. Kate ran the office and field staff; I headed up the engineering team. We all worked together very well. We worked hard, did what needed to be done and took plenty of risks along the way. It only takes one big lawsuit to ruin a company. It only takes resting on your laurels and thinking you are always going to be the "go to people" to have the entire industry pass you by. Our team always wanted to keep developing, keep progressing, keep making a real difference in our field. We did that. We made some great devices. We created and sustained a professional and comfortable work environment. We functioned as a team. We made money year over year and we - the owners - shared that profit with everyone, from the field reps to the IT team to the cleaning staff - we all shared in the fruit because we all shared in the labor. That was our way and it worked.

We were approached a few times through the years by investment groups who wanted to buy our company. Each time we listened to what they offered, but declined. We had a great thing going. All of us had made good money for many years. We enjoyed working together, still created useful products and were recognized experts in our field.

Almost two years before Dad passed away, a regional energy company came to see us. They were different. They offered us more money than previous suitors, and they offered us more stock in their company than the others. They made it very attractive for us to become a division of their company and keep making great tools for harnessing and distributing energy to consumers. To make a long story short, we took their offer and all four founders became wealthy. We shared a good portion of our cash with several employees who had been with us a long time. Shortly after the transaction Kate told me she wanted to resign from the company and help her parents sell their dry cleaning business for a fair price to finance their retirement. She trained her assistant and a well qualified new hire with previous business experience to take over her responsibilities. Our office team threw a fantastic and very heartfelt going away party for her, complete with cake, speeches and tears from co-workers who had become great friends over the years. After departing the company, Kate helped her parents get a good price for their business and set up their investments. This was classic Kate, always looking out for others. Even after her folks were settled into retirement, Kate found another outlet to help people through multiple volunteer roles.

As Kate expanded her volunteer work I continued working at the company. I had a two year earn-out agreement with the new owners, with penalties for early departure. When we went to the farm I had another 2 months left on my earn-out agreement. That meant in 2 months I could leave the company without penalty and not lose any stock. I also had a lot of built up paid-time-off, well over 2 months worth. The bottom line was this: I had enough money and enough stock that I didn't need to work for anyone else ever again. Kate and I could just continue investing reasonably well and travel to volunteer or to see family and friends. We could invest in something Brian wanted to do. If it succeeded, wonderful and if it failed, no big deal. I wondered if I really wanted to consider giving up that possible lifestyle for the life of a farmer. It wasn't like somebody handed us all this money. Kate and I worked very hard and took a lot of big risks for many, many years to attain this financial position. Money isn't everything, but I find that a lot of people who like to say "Money isn't everything" frequently gripe about not having enough money and even try to guilt other people into giving them money. Money is not everything, but it sure helps us do a lot of things.

What about organic farming? How do the economics work? I wanted to read accounts of both success and failure. I immersed myself in research when I wasn't on the job or doing things around the house. I learned a lot about organic farming, about agriculture in Okfuskee County, about soil, about rainfall and irrigation, etc. It became a quest for me. That is my approach, as usual - total immersion.

Chapter 5: Three Weeks To Be There

"Mike, if you want to take three weeks off, do it!," said Calvin. I had talked to him at the office about how I had not taken a vacation over 4 or 5 days long in more years than I could count. Calvin was one of the founders of our company all those years ago and a very close friend. He said that he, Danielle, Travis (the 4th founder) and the others at the office would be very judicious about calling me during those three weeks, and smiled. So, I emailed the others and let them know that I was taking those three consecutive weeks off. I didn't go into details. They were all very happy for me and replied with "It's about time!" and the like. Kate and I were both ready to devote some serious time to relaxing and seeing if we could come to a settled, firm decision about the farm.

That night Kate, Brian and I talked about what we could do with the three weeks I had off. Brian was doing some photography that he hoped would result in published images that generated some money. He said he could take plenty of pictures around the farm. Kate sounded excited about getting away and becoming very familiar with the environment of the farm. So, we agreed that we would pack our bags and head east to what might actually become our new home, our new business and our new life.

We pulled into the driveway and put our bags inside the house. I went out to the detached garage and opened the door. Dad's truck was there. I backed it out and put my car in the garage. I thought it was time to immerse myself in the life of the farm as much as I could. Inside the house I located Dad's desk and found his address book. I called the two guys who had worked for Dad for years and years to let them know that we were staying at the house. I didn't get into details with them either. I did tell them that we would finish out the current growing season and harvest and that we would weigh our options for the future. They understood. I made some more coffee with that crisp, clear well water. This time I had brought an abundant supply of fair-trade, micro-lot, organically grown coffee from our house as well as a good selection of teas; yes, most of them were certified organic. So, we had some really good coffee around the table as we talked about the next three weeks.

I said that what I wanted for me was a very free flowing time where I could follow my thoughts and feelings, talk through things with Kate & Brian at the table or the porch, and with God as I walked in the woods or the fields. I might be at a desk reading and writing most of the day or not at all. I was so used to deadline-driven work to make expensive and very specialized tools that I needed to just wake up and go where I was led. Kate and Brian agreed completely. They, too, wanted to be free to have all the alone-time they needed while understanding that we would surely want to come together to talk, to work, to eat and to pray. We all seemed to intuitively understand that while we had talked together and eaten together a lot, we really hadn't worked together or prayed together (all 3 of us) that much for years. I said that I was really grateful that we didn't have to make a decision quickly that would put us immediately in huge debt and huge financial risk. That said, we still didn't want to make a wrong decision and burn through a significant amount of our finances on something that ultimately failed.

That afternoon we walked through the house and I told a lot of stories; some I had not thought of for a long time. We walked around the outside of the house and of course more stories came to mind, which I shared. Kate and Brian each shared stories they remembered on our tour of the property. It was nice to relax and share stories from our history. It made "the farm" begin to feel more like "our farm".

That evening we drove into town for dinner. Afterward we took a drive to a ridge that I remembered going to when I was in my teens. It was a wonderful place to watch the fantastic sunsets we enjoy in Oklahoma. We all just breathed in the fresh air and took in the land and water around us. It was beautiful. Sure enough, as the sun dropped low on the horizon the sky and clouds took on brilliant shades of blue, orange and red with multiple textures in the clouds. Sure we saw them back home, but out in the wide open country the canvas of the sky seems limitless.

The drive back to the farm was relaxing. We put the windows down some and let the cool night air blow smells of wildflowers our direction. We could hear the sounds of bugs in the grass doing whatever it is they do at night. I could already feel myself starting, just starting, to unwind inside. We got to the farm, parked the truck and went inside. We were all ready to get some sleep so we made our way to bed and settled in. It didn't take long before I was out.

Chapter 6: Discovery

The next morning I gradually woke up. It was nice not to wake to an alarm clock or my phone ringing with a business task reminder or call. I looked over at Kate and she was still asleep. I made my way downstairs as quietly as I could. I found the tea, the kettle, milk… the most essential items for any morning of my life. I put the kettle on the stove, got the tea in my press pot, heated the milk and found my way to the sofa. I thought, "I don't have to be anywhere, or do anything today. That's nice." Of course, I then began to think about what I would do. We did have a big decision to make and I didn't want to drag out that decision unnecessarily.

I thought, "Well, what would be something simple and obvious to do?" I immediately remembered that Dad's clothes were still in the closet and in the drawers. It seemed like an important, simple and valuable thing to get his clothes together, set aside anything that stood out with sentimental value, and donate the rest to charity. That's what Dad would want.

I made my tea and went out on the back porch to enjoy the morning air and my tea that is such a valuable, simple and ever-present part of my life. The birds were singing, a light breeze was blowing and the sun was beginning to sparkle in the dew that covered the grass. I sank back into the chair and sipped my tea. I thought, "Now this is a great way to start my day." Of course, in Oklahoma not every morning is like this. We get some really cold mornings in winter, but not as many as our friends in the north. I thought, "Most of the year I could be out here in shirtsleeves or maybe a jacket and be just fine."

I finished my tea and then went back inside the house. Kate was up so I kissed her "good morning" and started our first pot of coffee for the day. I went upstairs, shaved, showered and came back downstairs. Brian was up and we all had breakfast together. We all agreed we wanted to have some alone time for the morning at least. Brian was going to take some pictures and Kate planned to read some. I told them I wanted to go through Dad's chest that was in his closet. We all went our way. I retrieved the chest from the closet and took it to the study. I got a fresh cup of coffee and closed the door.

I took the artifacts and the journal out of the chest and set them to the side. I knew in time I would want to figure out the stories I didn't know behind some of the items. What I wanted to get into were the two items at the bottom of the chest. There was a large, thick envelope with "Future Crop Plan" written on it. There was some mystery about that, but I had an idea that it was what Dad and Mom had in mind for the farm. The other was a box with "Celery Day" written on the lid. "Celery Day?" I said out loud. I thought, "What in the world does that mean? Knowing Dad it's either a joke or something deeply meaningful - and memorable - to him. I guess I'll find out." So I opened the box. Inside were letters... more like stories ... from many people in many places. The first one I read was the following.

> *Hello. My name is Sarangerel. I am from central Mongolia. I am the second daughter and fourth child of my parents.*
>
> *I have lived in the same region all 15 years of my life. We do not receive many visitors from far away. But, this year some British and American film makers came to stay with us. They were very nice and very interested in our way of life, even the most simple things.*
>
> *Our guests seemed to enjoy sharing our lives. None of them had lived in a ger before. Some had been on short trips to the forest in their homelands and slept in a very*

small ger they called a "tent". They were surprised by the taste of suutei tsai *or "milk tea", but said they enjoyed it. They ate our meat, potatoes, carrots and* ul boov *or "biscuits" with smiles.*

One night after dinner they showed us a picture of food from their home countries that they said was called Mongolian. We looked at the picture carefully, then laughed! There were things in the food we had never seen before! They began to explain tomatoes and celery to us, or at least they tried to. How do you explain a taste to someone? It can be difficult.

One of the group - Tom - decided to call a friend of his who was leaving southern Mongolia to join us. Tom said in the south that a few farmers were growing tomatoes and celery. He said he would ask his friend to bring some of each with him. We were interested in tasting these new foods, but not sure we would like them. As Mongols always do, we had offered our guests our best food. It seemed that Tom was offering us some of his best food, which was odd to us. He told us the tomatoes and celery would be a gift from him and the team to us and we were not in debt to them for it. We said that was okay.

When Tom's friend Shaun arrived we all greeted him. As he unpacked his bags he presented us with three tomatoes and a bundle of celery. We all took turns smelling the new vegetables. I remember how soft the tomatoes were and how hard the celery was. That night we cut up the tomatoes and celery and put them on a plate. Everyone got to eat them at the same time. I remember the strong taste of the celery leaves. Our American friends said in their home they don't usually eat the leaves unless they are in soup. I thought the taste was really good; strong, but good. The celery stalks made noise when we ate them! My brothers and sisters found it funny that our food was noisy. The tomatoes were okay, but I preferred the celery.

After a few weeks our friends had filmed many hours of life in our clan and it was time for them to return to their homes. On the last night we had together, I asked about the celery. I did not want to ask the price Shaun had paid, but I hinted that I was interested. He said it would be very expensive, more than most families would be willing to spend; and the same was true of the tomatoes. I knew that many people in America and England were more wealthy than most Mongols, so I asked our friends if they ate celery on many special occasions each year or only two or three times. They smiled and said where they live celery is not expensive and they eat it very often. They even said they like it in their "Mongolian" dishes. We all laughed.

Our friends left the next day. That day I thought about them and our conversations, about the many differences between where they live and where we live. They drank our milk tea which was different than their tea, and they liked it. We ate their gift of tomatoes and celery which were different than anything we had ever eaten, and we liked them. As I did my chores I wondered how else my life might change. Before our friends came I had no experience of certain tastes. Now I did. Maybe I could travel to Ulaanbaatar and discover what things there are to do and eat and see. That all seemed almost impossible, but interesting.

I did not want to forget the friends we made or the things they shared with us. Even if I lived the rest of my life in the same area, I wanted to remember the richness and the joy of discovery we had in those three weeks they were with us. I wanted a simple way to remember, a symbol. To me the sight, the smell and the taste of the celery they shared was a generous and thoughtful gift that gave me an experience that was new to me. That experience made me curious about what else might be true and available, but unknown to me. I decided to mark that day each year. I decided to call it "Celery Day" to remind me of what can be and that if I want something strongly enough, I can obtain it.

All three of us finished out that first day mostly by ourselves. I had read a few of the stories from the box and then went outside to walk the land and think. I walked past the barn and headed south down the road that separated the peach orchard from field 1, which was planted with cabbage. Further down the other fields were planted with beets, broccoli and potatoes. In the last field I saw a small segment of the field that had something else growing. From a distance I couldn't tell what it was. As I got closer I could see that it was celery. It was the "regular" green celery that we had bought at the grocery store forever. I had not been that far away from the house in at least 10 years, but the celery patch was new to me. I had never heard Dad talk about selling celery. Then again, we didn't talk that much about what he sold year to year.

All of the various types of plants I saw looked healthy at a glance. He and Mom had diversified the farm more about five years earlier. Prior to that they had grown two crops in addition to the peaches, of course. They would rotate the fields the two crops grew in. They had become convinced they needed to diversify the crops more to maintain the richness of the soil, and help the plants resist bugs and diseases. At that same time they had begun shifting away from using typical, commercial pesticides and fertilizers. They always tried to use as little of the chemicals as possible. As I recall, in the last three years they had not sprayed any synthetic chemicals on the crops. Dad said it was more work, but worth it for the sake of the food, the land and the people who would eat the food. He never had the farm certified as organic, but he knew he was at least heading in a better direction than he had been. That was classic Dad - just trying to keep improving and do what's right for other folks.

When I had rested for awhile near the property line I started walking back. When I came to the celery patch I thought of another one of those letters or stories from the box. It read:

"Sonkwe... Sonkwe!" my brother said in my ear over and over. I said, "I hear you Mwewa, okay? I hear you!" He started laughing and then I started laughing. It was still early, so we hushed ourselves. We knew it was the day. Oh, at last it was here! 161 days after we started, the day was finally here.

Our family has lived in the same village in Malawi for many, many generations. We have grown maize (corn) on our land for my entire life. We make nsima, which is a thick maize porridge that we shape into patties. We have nsima with beans or chicken sometimes. We like tomatoes, onions, cucumbers and green peppers with it depending on what is available. Fruit trees also grow where we live. We have always been thankful for the food we have and never complained about it. We have heard city people complain about our food when they visit and it is very off putting to us, insulting sometimes. In any case, we like our food.

Last year we made a journey to see some relatives in Zambia where they get more rain than we do. Father told us that our family there would welcome us and feed us food that was similar to our food. The journey was long but we enjoyed meeting so many cousins!

When the first meal was served we had nsima with some tomatoes and mild peppers... and something we had not tasted before. It was crunchy and bursting with flavor! I told my brother he sounded like a goat eating stiff grass when he ate it. He laughed and said I did too. Oh, it was such a nice flavor, and new to us. Celery.

Our cousins had been to South Africa some years earlier and they ate celery there. They bought some celery seeds and took them back to their home in Zambia. After much learning they succeeded in growing and harvesting it. They offered to send some seeds home with us and we said "Yes! Thank you!"

When our holiday was over we returned to our village with our seeds. Mwewa and I showed our mother and father the seeds we had been given and asked if we could try growing them. Father said, "Boys, the celery was nice to eat, but it takes 5 or 6 months to grow. It takes a lot of water to grow. I asked my cousin about it when we were visiting. How would we get the water for it in the dry months?" I said, "Father, Mwewa and I would only plant a small patch of celery. We could haul water from the river in buckets to water the celery in the dry months." Father clicked his tongue against the roof of his mouth and shook his head. He said, "Mmmmm. Do you know how much water it would take? Do you know how many trips to the river you would have to make every day in the dry months?" I looked at Mwewa, he looked at me. Mwewa said, "No, Father, we don't know. But, we want to try to grow this celery and eat it here where we live, in our house. We might even be able to sell it to other families!" Father smiled. Mwewa was always thinking of ways to earn money. Father said, "Before we start selling what we don't have..." and then grabbed us both by the neck and jostled us around as he laughed. Father continued, "Maybe we should grow some of this celery, yeah?" My brother and I shook our heads and smiled.

Father said, "Okay boys, I will let you grow a small patch of celery, but there are some things you need to understand." We were excited and eager to agree to whatever Father said. "First," he said, "I expect you to work on all the other crops and plants just as you always do. You cannot take time and work away from our other plants to work on the celery. Understand?" "Yes, Father" we said in unison. "Second, you both will be completely responsible for the celery. Your brothers and sisters, mother and I all have our work to do. We will not work on the celery. Do you understand?" "Yes, Father, we do" I said. Mwewa nodded in agreement.

Father sighed and looked at us. He said, "Very well, you may grow the celery in the southeast corner of the field behind our house. But, only use a 3 meter by 3 meter patch. And remember, when the dry season comes, you will carry each bucket of water. That patch will not be producing anything else this year, so give it your best if you really want to eat your own celery. I hope it works boys. I enjoyed the celery too." Father paused and said, "If the celery does not grow successfully, I don't know that I will be willing to let you try again next year. Your brothers and sisters are growing and we need to feed all of you, clothe you and pay your school fees. We need all of our land to produce, understand?" We both said, "Yes, Father. We understand." I said, "We will do anything necessary to make the celery grow. We will do it, right Mwewa?" Mwewa smiled and said, "Yes, Sonkwe, we will do it together. And, if it works, we might just sell some."

Mwewa and I got the seeds to sprout in 10 weeks. They required careful watering in that time, but we had plenty of water because it was the rainy season. We planted the seedlings approximately 15cm apart (really just the length of Mwewa's foot) in rows about 2/3 of a meter apart (really from heel to knee on Mwewa). This is what our cousin in Zambia told us to do, so we followed his instructions carefully. For the rest of the rainy season the celery grew nicely. Then, in April the rains were few as always. We noticed the leaves looked a bit withered one day and that is when we began going to the river to get buckets of water for our precious celery plants. At first, we only made one trip a day. As the month progressed we were making two trips a day, then three. In May we had one rain and in June none. We realized we had to make at least four trips a day - every day - to keep the plants healthy and strong. All the while we had to do our work on all the maize and other plants on our land. It was tiring. I wondered at times if celery was really worth all this extra work. Water is heavy, and our buckets are large. On rare occasion I dropped a bucket, or Mwewa dropped a bucket, and we had to walk all the way back to the river and start over. But, we kept reminding each other how good the celery was when we ate with our cousins. Then, we would laugh and call ourselves "the goat brothers" because of how we sounded when we crunched on the celery.

During the dry season Mwewa and I slept like our grandfathers. Mother said we snored all the time because we were exhausted at bedtime. It was funny, and I always wanted to go to sleep first. We would wake up and - after breakfast and our first chores of the day - we would go check our celery. One day we knew we were getting close to harvest time. The celery plants were just longer than my hand. We kept hauling water every day, four or five times a day as the soil needed in order to stay moist. When the plants were the length of my forearm, it was time. Finally, it was time!

Well, last night we went to sleep, knowing we would awaken to harvest time. Now, harvest was here. All of our work, our patience, our risk was going to finally pay off. And, today was the day. We would take the first stalks to Mother by mid morning and she would put them on our lunch plate! We would once again crunch those pieces of celery and taste the fragrant, unmistakable juice as it mingled with our maize and peppers and tomatoes. Ah! I can't wait to finally reap what we have sown and tended for so many months. Today is it.

Today is Celery Day.

As I walked back to the house I thought about what it would have been like to have grown up without celery. That made me laugh out loud actually. I said, "It's like these boys in Africa and the girl in Mongolia had made a discovery. I guess that's exactly what it was for them. A discovery." I laughed again, just because I probably had not even thought about celery in ages. It was just something that was always in the refrigerator, in cold salads, or soups. I honestly had never sat and thought about celery, at all. But, reading those stories made me stop and think. The people in the stories had never - never - had the sensation of the crunch of celery or the unique taste that it has. So, for them it was a real discovery of something new. One day they had no frame of reference for celery and the next day they did. And, it was not a small thing to them. I still did not understand how it was more important to them than just something different to eat. I still did not understand why Dad had some growing on the land, but not really enough to sell and make any significant money. I just shook my head and walked back to the house. It was nearing dinner time, and I wasn't about to miss dinner. Kate and Brian were cooking, so I knew it would be good.

Chapter 7: Time To Do It

The next morning we all sat down for breakfast. Brian had an idea he wanted Kate and I to consider. He said, "For the sake of discussion can we assume we all want to move here and run the farm as an organic farm? We could talk about the real-world details and requirements of living and working here. That way we would have a better idea of what we would be committing to. Does that make sense?" Kate and I both nodded our heads. She said, "That's a great idea. Passion and excitement are wonderful things for sure. I wouldn't want to live life without them. However, if we find ourselves in a very painful, or difficult or even impossible situation, our resolve will be tested. I think of resolve or commitment as "passion for the duration" versus passion that's just a whim that burns up in a moment. It's the lasting passion - the commitment - we need to make or not make." I agreed.

We had all seen farming from the periphery. We had heard about it from folks who did it. But, we had never done farming ourselves. It occurred to me that Dave and Marty (the two guys who had worked for Dad for many years) were going to be working that day. I said, "Well, I can't think of a better way to move from theory of farming to practice than to roll up our sleeves and get out there with Dave and Marty today. What do you say?" Kate and Brian looked at each other, then at me, with a slight look of surprise. But they both knew I was doing more than making a suggestion or trying to fill our day. I had issued a challenge. If they were remotely serious about actually, possibly becoming farmers, then they needed to put their hands on the plants, on the tools, in the earth - today. As the issuer of the challenge I had essentially committed myself to the task already. They both smiled and Brian said, "Yeah, we're in. It may be tougher than we think but we are here to make a decision. This makes sense, so let's do it!" When we walked outside the house, Dave and Marty were already at work. We walked to where they were working and said, "Hello." I then told them we wanted to work with them that day, that we wanted to do what they did, right alongside them. They looked at each other, then looked back at us. I'm sure they noticed that our hands did not look like we had done much hard work outdoors. Dave didn't take long to respond, "Sure. If you all want to work with us we are glad to have the help. Your dad was always a great worker. Even at his age he stayed right up with us when the task required it. He was always a great boss, too. I miss him." He caught himself, and said, "I'm so sorry. I don't mean to be insensitive to you all. I probably should not have mentioned him. Forgive me." I put my hand on his shoulder and said, "Dave, I'm glad you told me what you thought of Dad. He was something else to be sure. He always had good things to say about you and Marty." Both Dave and Marty smiled and looked at the ground. I looked at the ground, too. I think Kate and Brian did. I'm not sure because I found myself thinking how Dad loved the earth, the soil. He cared about the ongoing fertility and health of the soil. He knew that's where everything else on the farm got its life from. Marty broke the silence when he said, "Well, let's go to the barn to get you all some tools." We all headed to the barn and were issued our tools for the day.

As you might imagine, it didn't take long to realize I was not used to this kind of work. Kate and Brian had the same revelation at about the same time. But we were committed to see it through. Thinking about farming is not the same as farming. We were learning that by experience. Our hands got sore, our backs got sore, we were sweating, our shoes and boots were actually dirty... and we smelled the soil, we felt it in our hands, we felt the plants - the leaves, the stems - vibrant and thriving. We removed bugs and weeds that were working against our purposes and the plants' purpose. It felt new and yet like something almost instinctive. It felt like an investment of more than just time. Our sweat was now part of the soil.

We finished out the day with Dave and Marty. Their pace never seemed to change, but ours did. Dave was in his early 50s and Marty was in his late 30s. They were wiry, solid guys who found not only a paycheck but real enjoyment in the work. Dave had grown up in the area and worked on farms his entire adult life. Marty had served in the military for several years, worked as a welder and then moved his family near the farm when Dad hired him. It was a friend-of-a-friend connection, which was always Dad's preferred way to find new members for his team. Dave and Marty were veterans of the soil and it showed. We were greenhorns - started with a flourish and ended up fainting. Well, we didn't actually faint, but we wondered if we were. We said our goodbyes to them and went into the house for dinner. Right, dinner. Who was going to cook after all that work? We agreed that Brian and I would cook and Kate would shower first. We made a casserole of sorts that was okay. It wasn't something I'd make again necessarily, but I think it tasted better that night than it would have the night before. It was almost exciting to be that hungry.

When I got in bed that night Kate was already asleep. As I was reviewing the day's events I looked at my hands. They were really sore and I had two blisters develop and then break while working. I thought through all the different tasks we had accomplished and how much more there was to do. It occurred to me that when the day began I was determined to evaluate farming. By the end of the day, I realized farming was evaluating me. In my arrogance I thought I might even have something wonderful to bring to the farm and farming because of my engineering background. What I found was that simple tasks, with simple tools had worked me over… and taught me a few things. That reminded me of another one of Dad's "Celery Day" stories.

> *"Better Living Through Technology" I said. That was what I named my project that would make up most of the research for my master's thesis on applied technology. I wanted to help people in a very low income urban area become familiar with using the internet in ways that would benefit them for the long term. My advisor said, "That sounds like a noble goal. You get the research you need for your thesis, and the neighborhood folks get a dedicated room with better internet connections and the skills to use them."*
>
> *I set up a meeting at the local community center with the key leaders in the neighborhood. After the presentation I gave and a half hour of questions and answers, they agreed. I had already secured the funding, so I purchased the equipment right away. I arrived with multiple boxes in my car and was greeted by some excited folks who were staff and volunteers at the community center. We unloaded the car and spent the afternoon getting the equipment set up and tested. I knew I was going to make a big difference for these folks.*
>
> *We had our first class on internet basics the next day. All seven people who came were curious to see just how they could look at images and hear sounds from around the world, all with no "rabbit ear" antennas like many had on their TVs. I showed them how to get online. When they followed the steps, and pushed the "Enter/Return" button for the last time... their faces lit up. They could not believe they were seeing and hearing things produced all over the globe. I felt 10 feet tall, like inventors must feel who do something to help humanity live better. I didn't invent the computers or the internet, but I got to share the technology. I got to be the messenger, the teacher, the expert.*

Two days later in our next class I showed them how to find information for practical use, how to search for jobs, apply for jobs, find music they liked, etc. They were beginning to see the value of the internet not only as a novelty (at least among their friends and family), but as a tool for navigating life and sharing life with others. They were "getting it" and becoming converts to the online global community.

After several class sessions we were having lunch on a Saturday. A few of the volunteers and a staffer said they wanted to show me their community garden. I thought, "Why? What for?" But to appease them I said, "Sure, I'd be glad to see it." I was surprised what they had done with a vacant lot. They must have had a dozen different plants growing in their community garden.

They said if I worked with them in the garden, I could have some produce when it was ready. At the time I could use the food, but more importantly I could use their cooperation. I realized they were inviting me to join them in something that mattered to them. I didn't want to alienate them or do anything that would jeopardize my project, so I agreed to work with them in the garden.

Now, I did not really care for getting my hands dirty. One reason I went into the computer field was to work indoors. But, for the sake of the project I put my hands in the dirt. I figured they were putting their hands on the keyboards in my classes, and I was doing the same in their garden.

Over time, I listened to the conversations folks had while working the earth together. I started to engage in the conversations with them. I found myself feeling... connected... to the people and to the ground I walk on. These people were learning to see and hear things on a screen that could entertain them or help them practically. I was learning how to put my hands in the dirt around my feet to make a practical difference for them and for me. It was starting to become something I enjoyed, including washing up afterward (because I still didn't like having dirt all over my hands). They kept learning more about the internet and use of websites for business, professional development and fun. I began to see that planting seeds and caring for them can be for food, for a break from technology and for building friendships in a common task.

After I developed some skills they asked if I wanted to do a special job that made a big difference for one of the plants. They asked if I would wrap half of the celery from ground to foliage in order to "blanch" it. They said that depriving celery stalks of light near the end of their growing period made the celery less bitter and more nutty tasting. Some folks preferred their celery that way, while others preferred it more green and with a slight edge or bitterness to it. I followed their instructions and got half of the plants covered. As I preformed the task I was thinking how even in this seemingly small issue of growing such a common plant, they thought and acted like a community.

As my research project was coming to an end, we were also coming into harvest time for several crops. It soon came time to release the technology to the people who live in the neighborhood as the grant had specified. The computers and hardware would remain there and be the property of the community center. The harvest of the community garden would belong to these folks as well. I knew them now and was glad to share my technology with them. They shared their garden with me. In fact, the last thing we harvested was the celery. We tried some. Both the blanched and unblanched stalks had great crunch and flavor. They said I had earned all the celery I wanted. So I decided to take 6 bunches back to my apartment.

After saying our goodbyes that day, I drove home. It was on that drive that I realized I had gone to share something wonderful to me with strangers in need. In the process, those strangers shared something wonderful to them, with me. They shared their garden, their conversations, their laughter, their stories… their community … with me. I went to show them the world on a screen, they showed me human community right in front of me.

When I got to my apartment I made final preparations for a celebration of the end of my project with some friends. I opened bags and cans and arranged items on plates and in bowls. I had not planned to make celery a part of the celebration. But, after my experience with my new friends in our shared garden I decided to put both the blanched and unblanched celery on a plate with a few dipping sauces. My friends loved the taste. Some liked the darker green celery and some liked the lighter green celery. I shared the story of my project, the neighborhood community center that became a link to the world, the students who became friends, the community garden that became my learning ground and the humble plant that became a symbol of what love, nurturing and care can do for people, all people.

I decided to share the remaining celery with my friends. So, they all left with a bunch of their choice. I told them I wanted to remember what I had learned and not let it fade over time into some dusty memory. One of my friends laughed and shook his head. I asked him, "What? What's so funny? You have to share it with us. " He said, "As weird as it sounds, I think you should call today "Celery Day". It's a reminder of your whole experience man." We all laughed and agreed that henceforth, it would be known as Celery Day, a day of being grateful for things and for people, especially the ones we once took for granted.

Chapter 8: Transition

Most days for the remainder of my time off Kate, Brian and I worked on the farm with our hands. We used hand tools, we drove the tractor, we sprayed organic/naturally occurring pesticides and we ran the irrigation system. At night the three of us would talk about what we had learned. As we got to the two week mark, we started talking about whether the farm could be run more efficiently, more organically and if it would generate a livable income. That set Kate and I on a path to find out what market rates were for the crops growing on the farm as well as other crops we might put into our field rotation. That's when we discussed what to do with the small patch of celery. I didn't want to keep it going just because it was there. Knowing Dad, there had to be some connection between the celery patch and the "Celery Day" stories. Maybe it was a reminder to him of these stories? Maybe Dad had just really gotten a taste for celery in his later years? Kate and Brian both thought for sure there was some symbolic connection for Dad - and maybe for my mom, too - with the celery. I shook my head and said, "I think you all are right. That's not a celery crop big enough to make any serious money. So, either it was to share with other folks, or it was symbolic to Dad, or both." Kate said, "You know, why don't we keep it going for awhile and just see if it's something we want to do long term?" That seemed good to Brian and me. So, it was time to add celery to the list of plants we were learning so much about.

That third week on the farm we did a lot of research, a lot of walking, a lot of talking, thinking and some working. Our second to last day there, we sat down for breakfast. For me, I knew my decision. I was more quiet than normal, which Kate and Brian noticed. I think we all cleared our throats at about the same time, which of course made us laugh. I said, "So, do you all have anything settled in your hearts and minds about what to do?" Brian said, "Well, for me I do." Kate said, "I know what feels right on the inside for me." I said, "You know, we might need to rethink our wardrobes a bit... maybe get clothes more suited to... being farmers." And I just looked at my plate and scooped up some eggs and started eating. It was about that time that Kate slapped me on the shoulder and smiled at me. Brian shouted, "Yes! Yes! Woo hoo! This is awesome!" We made the decision to move and run the farm as an organic, family farm... our organic family farm.

We finished out our last couple of days at the farm and then drove back to OKC. The next day I made the announcement to the other founding partners of the company. They were surprised at first, and then all said they were really happy for me, and for Kate and Brian. They said I would be missed, but they would carry on. They said they wanted only great success for my family and me, not just monetarily, but in our family relationships and in this great, new adventure. Of course I then informed the CEO.

Over the next few weeks we did all the usual planning and distribution of responsibilities, exit interviews, etc. With each progressive step the reality that I was leaving the company I had helped found and run for over 20 years sank in more. At times it seemed like a very natural progression in life and at other times it seemed like I was watching a movie and I was one of the actors. Handing over responsibilities I had carried for so long to others felt both liberating and sad. I also knew I was going to leave behind my industry expertise. It would not take long for the company and the people in it to move on into new industry frontiers and my understanding would become more and more antiquated and eventually obsolete. What sustained me was the hope I saw in the farm for Kate, Brian and me.

When my last day came, it was only a little bittersweet. We had a nice long lunch, a few heartfelt speeches, laughter and a good number of tears, and cake of course. I finished the event by thanking everyone for being such a great team for so long. I told them from my heart that I would truly miss them all. As I walked down the hall - past the pictures and awards - carrying the required brown cardboard box with my last personal effects from my office, I remembered the early days of the company and all the changes we had been through. I walked past that first onsite childcare room where Brian had slept and nursed so long ago; where Kate had shown love in action for employees who were more like dear friends on a shared mission. I closed my eyes and let it soak in all the way that this was indeed the end of a chapter for me. More than that, I knew - down to my toenails - that it was time for me to leave and move on with the new adventure set before me. I was ready, very ready.

Chapter 9: Kids

Hi. My name is Bobby. I am five years old.

My dad likes tuna. He wanted me to try tuna but I did not want to. He said, "How about tuna salad?" I thought he meant a salad like Mom eats all the time but with tuna on it. That sounded yucky so I said, "Like Mom's salads but with tuna dumped on it? If I have to I will try it."

Dad tapped on his chin like he does when he is thinking. He smiled and said, "No. Tuna salad is a sandwich. And, best of all, it has alien fingernails in it! If we eat it we can gross out Mom and Rachel!" Just so you know, Rachel is my sister. She is six years old.

I said, "Yes! Let's eat alien fingernails in the tuna. Ha ha ha!" So, Dad made the tuna salad. He chopped up celery in little curvy pieces and said, "Those are the alien fingernails!" and wiggled his fingers around and made a goofy face with his eyes rolling around. So I did it to. We started kind of yelling and laughing "Ha ha ha ha" for a long time. It was fun.

He put the sandwiches on the table and we sat down. He said, "Are you ready?" I nodded my head. We both picked up our sandwiches and took a bite. The tuna was kind of like chicken and fish sticks put together, so it was okay. I asked what the crunchy stuff was. Dad said that was the alien fingernails. I made a goofy face at him and he made one at me like we were gagging. That is because Mom and Rachel will gag when we tell them.

So I tried tuna and celery all at one time. Dad talked to Mom later and I heard him say something about a "Two fer". I don't know what that is. I heard Mom say, "That's great! He tried new things finally!" Dad was so excited he said he wanted to mark the calendar so we would remember it. I ran into their room and said, "Let's call it "Alien Fingernail Day!" Mom thought that was really gross and that people might see that on the calendar and freak out. She said maybe he should just call it "Celery Day". Dad said that was okay. I still think "Alien Fingernail" day is better.

The end.

That story from the box not only made me laugh but underlined the importance of relating to kids where they are. I laughed because Brian and I always enjoyed a good joke and grossing out Kate, and Brian's female cousins. I remembered the challenges we had getting him to eat new foods at times. I remembered talking so many times with him about facing challenges, fears and disappointment with faith and courage. Sometimes the obstacles in my adult world of profession, family members facing addiction, politics, etc. seemed much bigger than Brian's problems of being teased at school, certain academic subjects and the teenage hair or clothing fad of the week. I had to realize that in his world those things really mattered. When I showed that I got that, that I cared and wanted to help, we had great conversations and we grew closer.

In deciding to move forward with the farm I made a focused effort to see it from his point of view and to talk about things I wanted to see changed in terms of how that met his needs. What was great was when I realized he was doing the same with me. He was maturing, behaving like a caring, compassionate and responsible adult who looked beyond his own immediate interests. That point was not lost on Kate either.

Once I left my career we made the move to the farm in a couple of weeks. We had no problem selling our house. We sold off most of our furniture and gave away other pieces to friends and family. It was really liberating to divest ourselves of things we had become used to but did not really need. We started loading the moving van and our cars on a Saturday morning and made the drive to the farm that evening. Dave and Marty came over the next day and we got everything unloaded. It took a week or so to get everything in place and functional, partly because we resumed working on the farm as well that week.

Several times that week the three of us looked at each other and said, "We actually did it! We are here. We are farmers now! Wow!" It was exciting and new and the potential for expansion and development of the farm seemed very real.

Chapter 10: He Got It

We talked some while we worked outside, but we had extended, profound talks in the evenings at dinner and afterward. We began to map out what it would mean to run our organic family farm. I used "mind maps" in my previous work a lot so I started a mind map on a big whiteboard which was a smart board as well. We had made an investment in this technology so we could capture and store ideas that we wrote and drew on the board. It was well worth the investment.

Before making the decision to run the farm I had wrestled with the idea of the farm being limiting. At the time I envisioned performing a handful of tasks at set times and otherwise not really knowing what to do with myself. I envisioned maybe converting to "mono-cropping" where we would raise one crop (at least one at a time) and get very efficient at it thereby maximizing yield and profits, blah, blah, blah. That was my view of farming. It was my interactions with the farm, with Kate, with Brian and with Marty and Dave that opened my eyes to the possibilities.

About the tenth morning after we moved into the farmhouse, I was out on the back porch with my pot of tea, enjoying the peace and quiet - except for the birds in the trees. I had taken a few of the unread stories with me to the porch. One resonated with me especially that day, when I had awakened thinking about what really could be on our farm.

> *I grew up with my brother in a single-parent household. Mom worked two jobs to keep our bills paid. She worked hard and we always knew she loved us. We laughed, we did homework… we had a good upbringing. Yeah, we always wondered where Dad went to when he left us, but we almost never talked about it.*

So, privately I missed Dad. Privately, I also got really tired of eating the following (almost exclusively): 1) cereal, 2) whatever fast food was cheap and plentiful that day and 3) whatever you could mix with hot water and eat immediately. Once in a blue moon Mom would bring home a couple of bananas or apples. They would get almost where you couldn't eat them, then she would take them to work or to the park to leave for animals.

I grew up with food being something that was necessary, but almost a bother. Food certainly wasn't anything very interesting or cool. I remembered first seeing the cooking and food channels on TV at a friend's house. I thought, "You have to be kidding! Who would watch that stuff?"

I went off to college, and I ate whatever was available in the cafeteria. It was more variety than I remembered growing up, but still just not a big deal to me. Then I met James. He had grown up in a household that was mobile. His dad worked for an oil and gas company. They had lived all over the world, in eight countries on five continents. That meant they ate food from all over the world. James and I hit it off and he asked me out. He took me to a South American restaurant that offered Venezuelan and Peruvian food. I wasn't sure I would like it, but I did. There were flavors and textures on those plates I never knew existed.

James and I got close and we began to get serious about our relationship. We kept eating at restaurants that featured food he knew from living abroad, but I had never experienced. As we approached graduation from college we started talking about the possibility of marriage. He proposed and I accepted. I was so excited to have the wedding and then get on with our married life!

One day about three months from our wedding day, as I pondered what married life would be like, I had a shocking thought, "Someone will need to cook our meals!" I did not want us to eat as I did growing up. I knew that was not a real option, for health reasons and also because of the food James had grown up with. It was the same food I had eaten with him for two years at numerous restaurants. As old fashioned as it may sound, I wanted to learn how to cook. So I enrolled in a cooking class. Wow! I am truly amazed at what I have learned about spices, meat, cheese and vegetables in this class. We had a whole class devoted to root vegetables - multiple types of potatoes, carrots and parsnips. Who knew all that can be done with roots!

Last week just to show us how far you can go with an ingredient if you try, our teacher showed us over a dozen ways to use celery in the kitchen. From ants-on-a-log, to salsa, to tuna salad, to braising celery as a side dish, we learned more about cooking with celery than I ever imagined possible. That class session made me think of the other potential in my life that I've not tapped because I just don't know it is there. It made me wonder how often I have settled for what was familiar because it was easy, instead of trying something new. It made me think of how many things in my life are familiar and maybe a little boring because I have never explored their potential. That experience so affected me that, to mark the occasion, I wrote on my calendar "Celery Day" as a personal reminder that - for the most part - life is what you make it, just like celery.

Funny, I saw in this lady's story how I had always seen the farm as a "given" in our family's life. I knew one day I would inherit it. I didn't really think much about the farm. When we visited it was nice, in a way, sort of like that old flannel shirt in my closet that I put on when I can first see my breath in the winter morning air. I might wear that shirt 3 times all winter, but it hangs in the closet all year. I saw the farm about 3 times a year and that was enough. I had no idea the potential in this place, this land, this family to do more with the farm than had ever been done. That night we had one of our best discussions after dinner about how to develop or expand the farm. We had really embraced this place and this way of life and were already seeking to make it our own, not just to carry on what had always been.

That next morning, while having my tea on the back porch, I was thanking God for the day, for another opportunity to think, believe and do here on this earth, for Kate and Brian, for the farm… both the legacy my parents left us and the future, yet to be planned, yet to be written. The future… plan. I remembered the large envelope in Dad's chest that had "Future Crop Plan" written on the front. I had forgotten all about that with all the other activity going on. It was tough but I waited until Kate was awake and in the shower before I went into our closet to get the chest. I was excited about seeing the plan, but I didn't want to wake her unnecessarily. I opened the chest and found the envelope in the bottom. I put it on my desk downstairs for reading after breakfast.

After breakfast Brian went with Dave and Marty and some other guys to put in a good, long day on the cabbage crop. Kate planned to give the curtains and furniture a good cleaning like they probably had not experienced in a long time, as well as researching "companion planting" of plants to help fight diseases and control pests, followed by finding a good deal on a new air conditioning unit (the one we had was old and you don't want to wait until mid-summer to buy an air conditioner where we live). I decided I would make a fresh pot of coffee and pore over the "Future Crop Plan".

When I opened the envelope I found several sheets of paper and a few dozen packages of organic seeds. Some of the seeds were for crops we had already planned to grow and some were not. I began to sort the seeds by category. I noticed that there were four types of celery seeds: green stalk (the one we were familiar with), yellow stalk (a self-blanching variety more common in Europe), smallage (very thin stalks with lots of leaves) and celeriac or "celery root" (a root vegetable like a parsnip). I had no idea there was more than long, crunchy, green celery but apparently there was.

As I read Dad's notes from the envelope I saw that he had envisioned moving to a fully certified organic farm in the very near future. Had he not become ill, I think he would have been ready to do just that at about the same time we were working the land. I always knew Dad was an insightful and intelligent man. What I did not fully realize was that this farmer in eastern Oklahoma was very much aware of trends in food production and consumption and had plans to vigorously pursue the market in organics in Oklahoma City, Tulsa and surrounding areas. He had a vision for the farm and for his local community. He didn't see himself as "just a farmer trying to make ends meet". No, he saw what he and Mom had built as alive, vibrant, relevant and necessary to meet a real need. He had even written in his notes, "Everyone has to eat, and they may as well eat well!" He did not see himself as "some farmer in 'fly over land'." He saw himself as participating in life to the fullest, including in his career. He was providing quality food for people and he saw great potential for everyone involved to get what they wanted.

I sat at my desk with my eyes closed. My respect for Dad had grown as I read his notes. He got it. He got the market. He got the farm. He got the potential that was here. He never once pressured me to see it. He knew if I wanted to explore it for myself and my family I would. He knew if I got quiet, humble and receptive enough - and God was leading this direction - I would hear it. Sometimes we have to get down to the simplest of things to find peace and meaning in life… or to recover that peace and meaning.

I'm clenching my teeth, driving to work. Inside I'm rolling around between despondency, anger, fear, abandonment... and wanting to just somehow push "reset" on... everything. All this turmoil is making me fight off tears. Tears? I don't want to cry, especially when I'm driving! It would be hard to see, messy and maybe others would wonder what's wrong with me. Well, that's how life has seemed for awhile altogether - hard to see, messy and people are wondering what's wrong with me.

Let me back up. Life seemed a lot more together and understandable for years. My spouse and kids were healthy, none of them were doing drugs and we were all moving forward in school and professionally. We had close family and friends. We had friends we got together with to talk, pray, study, worship and grow spiritually. My job was going fine. Everything was good.

Over time my job started changing into something that was not sustainable. For the first time in many years, I wondered if I should look into a career change. At the same time my older son began to deal with a serious illness. I wanted to fix that, but couldn't on my own. It seemed like the group we gathered with to grow as followers of Jesus had begun to drift. As time went on, I started wondering if I was really doing enough to carry out what Jesus wanted me to do... in anything.

I realize there are folks who deal with a lot more immediate, painful issues, like not having any food, not being able to pay rent, their spouse beating them, family stealing from them to buy drugs, the death of someone very close, and on and on. I know my problems weren't life threatening, but they were real problems for me and those I'm closest to. I needed answers and direction.

After 9 months of prayer, meditation, throwing up my hands, repenting, and wallowing in my frustration, I was at the end of my rope. This is when I was driving to work, teeth clenched, feeling really clueless, yet responsible to know what to do for me and my family. I pulled into the parking lot at work. I turned off the engine and sat there. I must have sat still and quiet for 3 minutes, but it felt like an hour. I was looking for the right words to say to God. I finally just said, "I feel like I don't know anything any more. I am willing to do anything you want, but I just don't know what that is now. I should know better by now. I should be the stalwart spiritual, social, financial and every-other-thing-in-life guide for my family. Instead I feel like someone who is just trying not to do anything stupid today."

Silence. I sat in absolute silence in my car. It was as if I could not only hear but see the noise in my heart and mind. It was like seeing a huge piece of paper with endless scribbling all over it. Lots of motion, but no progress. Noise but no intelligible sound that mattered. So many questions and expectations and frustrations. Why? Why am I feeling this?!?

I said, "I am willing to do whatever you want." And I shut up. I realized the one big question - the one that mattered most of all - was just that, "Lord, what do you want?" I thought on that, meditated on that for just a few seconds. What rose up inside of me was this - "Be thankful". Not, "Be thankful for X"; just, "Be thankful." It caught me off guard. I thought about that. Then I smiled. I felt the chaos start leaving me. In a matter of a minute, life for today became really, really simple. Be thankful.

I started by saying "I am thankful for my job." I said that I was thankful for my car. I said I was thankful for my clothes, my shoes, my co-workers and my family. It became a wonderful thing just telling God what I was thankful for that day. I realized that this most basic spiritual discipline was sorely lacking in my life.

When lunch rolled around, I opened my lunch bag and found my plastic container of raw veggies, my sandwich and a piece of fruit. As usual, I opened the veggie container first, ready to be thankful. For a few days in a row I had had carrots alone in the container. I was ready to be thankful for carrots again. When I opened it, there were carrots, but there was something else. Celery. I said, "Thank you Lord for celery today!" I got thankful for my celery and just kept on thanking God for everything. That altered me. So, I altered my calendar and declared that day "Celery Day" so I remember to be thankful even for the so-called little things.

Chapter 11: The Familiar

We finished out that Fall with a nice harvest and sold our produce to buyers Dad and Mom had sold to for years. We did take some of our produce to friends in Tulsa and OKC. They had been curious about what we were doing and had not yet made it to the farm. We enjoyed telling the story of how we made our decision and showing them the tangible results of our family's work and the work of some hired folks who felt pretty close to family already. The experience we were having with the plants and the land was new and wonderful for Kate, Brian and me. What was familiar was the warmth, the commitment, the genuine friendship of the people we worked with. We felt the bonds between the three of us growing deeper and stronger as well. We had been living on the farm for five and a half months at this point. It was starting to feel like our new normal.

As we got the farm prepared for winter, we looked forward to some shorter days of work and more time to be indoors, reflect, talk and all those other things that fit with winter. We had come to know Dave and Marty and their families pretty well. We had them over for dinner and had a great time. The six of us parents talked about the farm, about where we saw the farm going in the next few years, about county politics, about extended family and favorite holiday traditions. Brian got along well with Marty's kids. Brian had also met some of the folks his age in the area and enjoyed hanging out with them. Kate had met two ladies at the library she hit it off with. We were building relationships with local people and those relationships were good.

We also missed friends back in OKC. We talked on the phone and video-chatted with them at times. But, that is not the same as seeing people face-to-face. As winter progressed, and our hands weren't as busy with outside work, we found ourselves thinking and talking about our old friends. One night Kate mentioned one of our favorite restaurants in Uptown OKC that we had not been to for months. I actually got quiet and thought about their blackened salmon with lump crab meat, covered with a light cream and caper sauce, with risotto and sautéed mushrooms… followed by moist, spicy bread pudding with a light caramel glaze and a perfect cappuccino. After I regained consciousness, I eloquently stated, "Yeah, me too." Brian commented on how he missed the coffee shops he and his friends frequented and sometimes played on open mic nights. We sat there quietly for a few minutes. I said, "Well, let's go visit in a couple of weeks. How about that?" They agreed. We went to bed that night and got a good night's sleep.

The next morning I was researching farm-to-table restaurants within two hours of our farm when I got a text from Calvin that read, "Hey Mike. Give me a call when you get a chance." I knew Calvin well enough that he was not reaching out to me for purely social reasons. For a second I wondered if perhaps he was wanting to join us on the farm. After all, he had done well financially and I thought he might be interested in a career change. In the next moment I thought he probably just had a question that the team had worked on as best they could but they were stuck and he thought I might have some insight that could get them un-stuck again. I finished my coffee and went out on the porch.

"Hello this is Calvin," came the familiar answer on the other end of the phone. I said, "Hi Calvin, it's Mike." "Miiiike! How are you man?" asked Calvin. I said, "I'm fine. Good to hear your voice. I got your text of course. What's up?" He replied, "Well, Mike, I know you are really enjoying the farm and have found a good groove with that. But, we had an opportunity come our way that I wanted to float by you." I said, "You mean you have a technical question?" Calvin paused for a few seconds, then said, "Well, more than a question. I think we may be in a little over our heads. I think we would really benefit from your engagement on this project, at least at some key points." It was my turn to be quiet, for several seconds. I said, "Well, I won't make any promises, but go ahead and give me the 3 minute overview." Calvin knew I always wanted people to condense their view of a project into a concise statement about the problem or need and specific options to meet that objective. He laid it out for me. It was an opportunity we had worked on a couple of years earlier, but the client got cold feet before we could start making a prototype. We - I mean the company - still had the research we had done on file. Calvin said, "I know you led the initial research on this and I think you could help save us some serious time on this project, if that would fit with what you are doing now."

Winter is the slow time on our farm. So, I knew I had the time but I just didn't know if I had the interest, the heart for it. I told Calvin I would think about it and get back to him the next day. That night I talked with Kate about it. She said, "Well, if you have the interest in working on the project I'd say go ahead. I just wouldn't want you to get part way into it and realize you don't want to continue. You aren't a quitter Mike. I don't want to see you get stuck with something you don't want to do. Also, we are still really early in operating this farm. We are doing our research and preparation to plant in the spring as a fully organic, sustainable farm. We have made good progress on that I think, but I don't want us to have a misstep in our first year. So, if you do it I will support you, but I will also pay attention to you, because I love you. And, I care about this new venture being successful." I said, "Thank you, as usual Babe. I'll get quiet and check in on this. If I have peace about it I'll do it. If not, I won't."

The next morning I was having tea on the porch. I had to wear a heavy jacket but it was worth it to be outside. As I sat still, clearing my mind - listening in my spirit - I had a sustained peace about working on the project. So, I called Calvin and told him I was in. He emailed me the files from the previous work we had done on it and I began to remember how the story unfolded. It was exciting to see the potential this product could bring to the natural gas industry. We set up a conference call for the next morning at 9am. After breakfast, Brian asked if I wanted to go with him into town and I said I would have to pass. He asked why. When I told him, he seemed troubled. I told him I wanted to know what he thought. He essentially voiced the same concerns as Kate. I assured him this was just a special project and it would in no way hinder what we were doing with the farm.

The conference call went well. I was able to contribute some history on the last time we looked at this project, as well as potential pitfalls and some recommendations on the best way forward. The team at the office knew what to do next and dove into the project. I put the project aside and immersed myself in the farm again 100%. A few days later, I got a call from Calvin. He said, "Hey, key decision makers from the client's office are coming in for a meeting on Friday. They remember working with you before. Is there any chance you could be here for the meeting and dinner afterward? I know that may be too much, but I wanted to ask you, Mike." I wrestled over this. Kate and Brian were supportive but I could tell they wondered how much time and energy this project would ultimately take and just where this would go.

I went. I wore my favorite suit, which I had not worn in quite awhile. Like every professional, I had done my research, rehearsed key points I needed to make in the presentation and on the drive to the office I got in the right frame of mind to present, and to win. It was like old times, and it was exciting.

The team and I assembled in the conference room for a final review of pertinent specifics before the prospective clients arrived. Calvin met them at the front desk and walked them to the conference room. When I saw them face-to-face I remembered more specifics from our past meetings, their roles, attitudes, etc. I was surprised at the rush this was for me. I had done presentations so many times that they had become common; valuable, interesting, but common. This did not feel common after just a brief time away. The lights were dimmed and I began the presentation. I was the expert regarding the innovations put into a key, new product and our - I mean the team's - new product would help the client. After the presentation and a brief question and answer period, they said they wanted the product in the field as soon as possible. I shook hands with their CEO and the deal was done; we just needed the legal teams to draft the contracts.

Afterward we went to a very nice dinner with the new clients. After dinner, my former CEO pulled me to the side and said, "Mike, I want you to know that I really appreciate your effort and expertise on this project. I honestly don't think we could have won this business without you." He made a few other comments that were positive as well. I have to admit, that felt pretty good. I drove from the restaurant and got a large coffee for the hour and a half drive back to the farm. That drive gave me a lot of time to think over what had transpired and what it really meant to me.

I got home to the farm and Kate and Brian were still awake. They asked how things went. I said, "The presentation and discussion went well. It felt like what I was doing was going to make a difference. And, we left the room with the deal!" Kate and Brian both smiled. Then, they looked at me with a question in their eyes, but not in their mouths. I don't think they wanted to ask me outright. I said, "It felt good to be back in the game, to present and to win." Brian asked, "Had you missed it? I mean did you realize you really missed the high-stakes, big-dollar innovations and rubbing shoulders with major players in the energy industry? Was all that appealing to you?" I thought for several seconds, not wanting to over or under state my feelings. Kate could tell there was more to the story. She asked, "What happened? You look like there is still something rolling around inside you." I said, "Well, the CEO asked me point blank if I had thought about coming back to the company. He said they would be glad to have me back and would make it worthwhile." Brian and Kate both looked at me. We were all quiet for a few seconds. I looked at them both and said, "It was sort of exciting, but not satisfying, not like it used to be. It was okay but I didn't really miss it. I missed the farm. I missed the feeling at the end of a day's work here. I missed thinking about how we would work to make next Spring better than ever." Kate and Brian just looked at me, waiting for closure. I said, "I told him 'Thanks, but no thanks.' I'd found the path for me at this time in my life and I was going to stay on it with my family." They smiled and we hugged. It was something of a test and it further solidified my resolve to stay the course with the farm.

I knew some of the folks back at the company saw what I was doing with the farm as beneath me, as too common a thing for someone with my training and expertise to immerse himself in. Well, they were wrong. They thought food was just common and ordinary. They didn't think about how food is produced and made available to people. I had come to see food production as something familiar and yet noble. My mind went to another of those stories from Dad's chest.

*"We have to wire it. So plan on six weeks of liquid food,"
said my doctor. I was in enough pain and on enough
pain medication that I wasn't thinking ahead. So I just
drifted off to sleep, as they prepared to wire my jaw
shut. What a price to pay for not paying attention at a
job site. One bad fall - or, like my best friend Sherman
said, "Really a very bad landing" - radically altered my
plans for that summer.*

*When I began to come to after the procedure, I was still
on a lot of medication. As my head began to get clearer,
I started to feel hungry. That is when my liquid diet
began. Broth, smoothies, shakes, tea, water, juice...
repeat. It was just what I had to do, and I was glad to
have those liquids for the first few days. Then, I began
to get really, really tired of the same few things, over
and over. I missed flavors and textures, chewing and
crunching and rolling foods around in my mouth. I lost
weight. I got tired of trying to talk to people. They could
understand most of what I said. My brothers made sure
to poke fun at my speech problems every time Mom
and Dad were not around.*

*As we entered the last three days of my liquid diet, Mom
said when the wires came off I could have mashed up
bananas and yogurt for a few days, then some
additional foods with a little texture for the next few
days. She asked what I wanted to eat after I got that
first week of solid food under my belt. I told her I wanted
her famous chicken salad with grapes and celery. That's
always been my favorite thing Mom makes. Oh, I
thought about eating real food again all the time! I even
dreamed about chicken salad!*

*After six weeks of no solid food and a week of soft food,
Mom's chicken salad with crunch celery was like my
birthday and Christmas all in one. I ate my first small
sandwich with the biggest, goofiest smile you have ever
seen. All the tastes were wonderful. The texture of the*

bread and the chicken were satisfying. What surprised me was how much I loved the crunch and taste of the celery. Who knew I could miss celery so much? I even asked Mom for some more celery on the side. I ate some raw celery and loved the taste and the crunch. It's like that song from the 70s that Counting Crows also sang, "You don't know what you got, 'til it's gone."

That night I went to bed and just laid there thinking. Life can change so much, so fast. It's easy to get bullheaded pursuing something you want and forget to be thankful for what you have. I thought of a lot of things, including how life itself (at least as we know it) doesn't last forever. My fall could have been worse; I could have died, but I didn't. The people in my life can be here today and gone tomorrow. Jobs, houses, cars, girlfriends, friends, neighbors… everything and everyone is subject to change. I wondered what - if anything, or anyone - was really, really permanent, stable… like bedrock. I realized I had not actively thought about God for quite awhile. I had been really busy doing my thing, you know? I was just living, like everyone else it seemed. But, I found myself thinking things I had not thought for a long time. I said out loud, "God I don't want to wander around anymore. Life is too precious and I get that now. I want to get it right, with you first and foremost, then with the people closest to me. I will seek the truth about you. I know you will help me find it, to find you." I've been on a good journey ever since.

That date on the calendar meant so much to me. It was far more than my return to eating what I want - and being thankful for it. It was the day that I made a commitment to myself and to God not to take life or anything in life for granted, because it's not granted. I wanted to permanently etch "the glory of the common" in my life. So, I declared that day "Celery Day". And, that day remains a reminder to me every year and in fact every day.

Don't wait 'til it's gone to know what - and who - you've got.

After finishing that presentation I was ready for a break, so we did go ahead with that weekend visit to OKC. It was nice to see longtime friends and to eat at familiar restaurants. The coffee shops were great. We all did some shopping with our friends. It was really nice. But, it wasn't home anymore.

Chapter 12: Owning It To The Root

As part of gearing up for Spring planting the three of us talked specifically about how much of which crops to plant. After breakfast one day we cleared the table and all got our notes. I also brought the "Future Crop Plan" envelope to the table. Kate and Brian had both read Dad's notes and seen the seed packets in it as well.

We talked about broccoli, cabbage, radishes, snap peas, eggplant, potatoes, tomatoes, Swiss Chard, spinach, beets, strawberries, okra, sage, basil, asparagus, rosemary and celery. As we worked through our decisions we all agreed we were surprised by the four types of celery we found in both Dad's notes and in seed form. If we had ever heard of anything but the long, green stalk celery we certainly didn't remember it. Brian had learned that celery seed comes from smallage and is valued for health benefits and well as its intense flavor. Smallage provides a lot of leaves which are also valued for their intense flavor. Kate was interested in the yellow stalk or "self blanching" celery that is favored in Europe and celeriac. She had collected some recipe ideas for both of those and thought there was real potential in our regional market for them. So, we agreed to plant all four varieties.

We took great care to plan out our patches of various plants. Some seed we put into the ground, other seed we let sprout and then put the sprouts in the ground. We had groups of plants that liked a lot of water, some that liked less water, some that needed really quick drainage, higher pH, lower pH, more manure, less manure… you get the idea. We had put a lot of time and energy into our research and planning over the winter and we were determined to pay attention to the details and get it right. We were all too aware that we needed to give our plants every advantage and minimize the disadvantages they had to deal with.

We were excited to put in our first crops when the time came. We knew we were farming last summer and fall, but those were crops that we had inherited. This spring's crops were crops of our choosing, for good or for ill. We felt this new way of life had become part of our bones now. We owned the farm legally before, we owned it emotionally now. Our investment was accumulating and our human-capital investment this season was going to exceed what we had done when we were just getting started.

In the midst of all the excitement and work, I noticed Brian seemed just a little detached at times. I chalked it up to being in his early 20s and having had so many diverse interests for the last few years that he just needed to focus. I thought he just needed to stay the course and let his commitment and passion for this way of life, this business, get deeper in his bones, in his own way. Kate noticed the same things in Brian, especially being quieter at meals.

About a week after we got all the seeds and sprouts in the ground we were sitting out on the front porch after dinner. Somewhere in the middle of my coffee I asked Brian how he was doing. Understandably, he said, "I'm fine." I said to him, "I asked because you seem a little distracted or detached the last few weeks. Your mom and I didn't want to pry, but we do want you to know we love you and we want to help if we can." He sighed and said, "I know you both love me and care. I've been trying not to just be a whiner or look like I'm wavering on the commitment to the farm and to you all. I am all in; I want that to be clear." Kate and I nodded our heads. Brian continued, "I just think … I guess like you say the 'new' has worn off of farming. I also miss my friends more than I thought I would. Some of them will be doing fun things on spring break this semester and I will be here. Aaaggh! I hate even saying these things, because it sounds like 'Brian the Butterfly' losing interest again." That was when he teared up. Man, he fought it. But, those deep feelings tied to how we see ourselves are going to be dealt with one way or another.

I got choked up listening to and seeing my son struggling. But I wanted him to talk out what he was really feeling and what he wanted without my interrupting. He dried his eyes and said, "I want you both to know with absolute certainty I am here. This is our farm, our business, our life now. I realize I probably just need to spend some more time with my new friends here and that will displace this frustrating sense of, I don't know, loss or whatever. When you went back for the business meeting Dad, the thought went through my mind that we all could just go back to life as it was, you know? We could still sell the farm, get a lot of money, I could start a coffee shop with Ben and Terrance and you both could plant a nice garden in the back yard. That lasted about five seconds. Then, I thought about what we would give up to go back to what was comfortable and predictable. I said 'No! No way am I going to just walk away from the farm. No way am I going to leave both of you to do this without me. No way am I going to be the flaky dude who just wanders through life self-absorbed and looking to be entertained and air conditioned all the time. I want - **I want** - to put my hands in the earth. I want to sweat and get sore working. I want us to build something that's a great business, but more than that. So, I am all in. I think I just needed to get that out there. Now that I have, I'm more than okay."

Kate said, "Brian, I'm glad you shared what is going on in you with us. I've had a moment or two when the thought of going back to life as I knew it sounded pretty good. But like you, I looked deeper inside and I counted the cost of staying with the farm and working it with you and your dad. I think it's healthy and freeing to acknowledge there is a cost to doing anything, and it will cost you the time and energy you could have invested in other things, other relationships. I counted that cost and my resolve to stay the course with you two and this farm just went deeper in my bones than before. That said, I do think you need a couple of evenings a week where you go somewhere with other people to build those relationships and have some fun. I know your dad and I are the most fun people you know, but…" We all burst out laughing at that point.

A couple of weeks later Brian got a message from one of his friends who was a senior at the University of Oklahoma in Norman. He and some friends were planning a camping and canoeing trip on the White River in northwest Arkansas over spring break. They invited Brian to join them. Kate and I said that if he wanted to go he should go and we - along with Dave, Marty and the others - would keep the farm moving along just fine. As it turns out, it was on that trip that Brian met Violet, a senior studying sustainable agriculture who was looking for a summer internship on an organic farm. We were glad to help her with that. I'm pretty sure Brian was even more glad than Kate and I were. They began spending more and more time together and soon there was a beautiful, sprout of a relationship they both enjoyed. The question was where it would go, what it would become. The three of us talked about that more than once around the table and on the back porch, and even as we worked. The day came to talk about it with Violet as well. Both Brian and Violet seemed to really understand that they had to decide what they wanted in the relationship and nurture it, just like the plants we all love working with.

> *I looked up from my new favorite book just as she said, "Julia, no baby come this way!" She was chasing her toddler who was trying to escape from the kiddie area of the park and go over where the big kids were playing. Of course, Mom caught the toddler who was not very happy to be apprehended and kept from the big shiny*

slide. So, the age-appropriate discussion began about how there is a special area at the park just for her and other kids her age where they can have fun and not get hurt. If you are a parent you know the conversation well. If you were ever a kid, you may remember the same discussion.

Of course, I then remembered having that conversation with my toddlers. I also remembered my own kids when they got into their early teens and wanted to go and do things my husband and I were not ready for them to do. I don't mean growing pot in the basement. I mean wanting to go on a road trip with their 18 year old, "been in rehab a couple of times" cousins for 4 days. I mean working on uncle Frank's alligator farm for the summer. Neither happened, and we talked about why.

Funny how that discussion changes over time, but the idea is the same. "This is good for you, that is not, or at least not right now" is the message. That goes not only for activities but for food. If you have ever tried to feed a small child something they didn't want (think kids in high chairs) you know that they may capitulate and eat it, fuss for awhile and then eat it, scream and cry and then eat it, scream and cry and slap at the spoon and the bowl and then eat it, or freak out completely as if you were a mad scientist experimenting on their tastebuds and not eat it at all. Why do we deal with this amount of difficulty instead of just feeding them what they want when they want it? Simple: we know what is good for them. Their long term health is more important to us than their short term gratification. Right?

My sister had her two little ones and her teenage son Wayne when she came over to our house last 4th of July. It was good to see them again after a few months apart. They got settled in the spare bedroom and in the upstairs game room (for Wayne of course). Then they came downstairs for the pre-cookout grazing session in the kitchen. As we talked and caught up on the last few months, I noticed Wayne didn't say much. Teenage boys don't usually talk much to their aunts, but this was different... he reminded me of our son Matt, just a handful of years before.

Our son Matt was one of our boys who wanted to work on the alligator farm and wanted to do the roadtrip with the questionable cousins one summer. After that summer Matt began to withdraw from activities and people, little by little. He stayed away from home more and was always in his room when he was home. My husband and I talked so many times about whether we needed to ask more questions or get more involved with Matt. He was getting older and needed more freedom to make his own choices, we thought, so we didn't press the issue. His grades suffered. By now you can probably write the rest of this paragraph. One day we came home and found Matt unresponsive on the floor in his room. We called 911 and the ambulance came. As with many, the interventions in the ER were successful and Matt survived. It was a very close call from an overdose of prescription drugs. Matt has been mostly clean and sober now for 4 years, with a couple of relatively brief relapses. Our relationship with him is better than ever. He's working and has his own apartment now. His story could have ended very differently.

So, back to Wayne on 4th of July. I saw a vacancy in his eyes. It was familiar. So, I encouraged Wayne to say 'Hi' to the other guys outside while his mom and I talked. I didn't waste any time with her. I said, "You remember what happened with Matt? I'm not trying to be nosy, I'm trying to help. I see some concerning things with Wayne. Do you see them?" She began to cry, "Yes, I do, but I don't want to push him away by prying into his private life, you know? If his dad were still around maybe he could. I don't know." I volunteered both my husband and me to talk with Wayne. I said, "Kids take a lot of nurturing. We didn't engage enough with Matt, even when we saw signs of problems. Don't make that same mistake with Wayne. Let him know you care.

Show him you care by listening. We will show him we care by listening."

Since then Wayne has been on a couple of fishing trips with my husband and sons. I heard the conversations were good and pretty substantive. Matt and Wayne have become closer and talk on the phone sometimes and text message a lot. My sister says Wayne has started doing a little more around the house, sometimes without even being asked. That was a surprise. I told her I wanted that to rub off on my guys! The bottom line is, it seems Wayne has made a turn. I think it had something to do with people who love him taking action on that love, showing we are thankful for him in our lives.

Children are a huge responsibility and they require huge commitment, lots of time and energy... if you want to do it right. You can't guarantee the outcome of their lives, but you can do what you need to do to be a real, true parent for them. Kids take work, lots of work. You get tired, you cry... and you laugh, and hold them close. Children require nurturing of different kinds at different stages of development. In order to do your part - day after day, year after year - you have to sit down and really think, pray and soak in the reality of what it means to be a great parent. Parenting isn't a competition for some badge or trophy. It is preparing your children to live successfully when they no longer live under your roof. You have to get settled on what that success looks like and what you will do - not imagine - actually do, and say, to your children to train them how to live.

This may seem odd, but I will share it with you anyway. I like to garden. The activities of gardening help me relax and understand the rhythms of life. A great garden does not make itself. I have to tend it, nurture it. I have to understand enough about each type of plant to give it what it needs to flourish.

Last year I learned that some fellow gardeners were trying to grow celery. They said it is one of the most challenging plants to grow. Well, I decided to take the challenge as well. I learned that celery has very specific requirements in order to grow and produce a good tasting stalk for eating. As I watered, and monitored temperature and shade, the plants grew. I paid close attention to soil moisture and watched for signs of pink rot fungus, fusarium wilt or leafminer larvae. I wrapped the stalks on a few of them at the right time to blanch them. After all that work, today is the day. Today is the day I get to enjoy the celery that took so much effort. You know, it's like enjoying times with your kids after all the work of caring for them, letting them be in the sun, shading them when needed... tending, caring, nurturing. Today is Celery Day... the day all the work and commitment is rewarded. Thankfully with our kids, we get rewarded over and over and over for the investment we make in them.

Chapter 13: Never Thought I Would Miss It

The spring season went well for us. We dealt with bugs of several kinds, had a few diseases attack a couple of our crops and had an irrigation malfunction in the beet patch that resulted in loss of about a third of our beets. We planted all four varieties of celery and they did well. We didn't have to deal with blight or root-knot nematodes in any of our celery patches. We were thankful that the plants were as healthy and vigorous as they were. For us, we followed what we have found to be sustainable, fulfilling and effective principles for not only farming but life in general that spring and summer. We did our homework, prayed for wisdom and sensitivity to God's leading and then worked as smart and as hard as we needed to.

When the time was right we harvested some of each crop to eat ourselves and ensure that what we wanted to sell to others was top quality to our own taste. We eventually got to the celery patches and harvested some of each of those. We made chicken salad, all vegetable salads, crawfish étouffée, mirepoix, soups and anything else we could find recipes for to try each type of celery. Each had its own characteristics that worked very well for each dish. We finally experienced for ourselves these varieties of celery on our own plates and now there was no going back. Celery would no longer just be the variety we grew up with, particularly just as something to hold dip at parties or peanut butter for an afternoon snack. No, those days were gone for good. We knew there was more by experience now. It took faith in what Dad had researched and believed for us to invest our land, our effort in growing these celery plants, most of which we had not eaten. Now, we not only enjoyed these celery varieties ourselves, but we wanted to share them with others so they could enjoy them.

One night after a particularly delicious meal that involved our own celery, I laughed out loud. Kate and Brian both asked what I was laughing about. I said, "You know, sometimes things just strike me as funny, especially when I think of trying to pack a great lesson or experience I've had into a few words for someone else." Kate said, "Okay. Such as?" I said, "I'm sitting here thinking about celery. Celery! A year ago I never thought about celery. Who thinks about celery?" I laughed. They saw what I meant. How would we tell our friends back in Oklahoma City that we have come to appreciate … celery? Or, how can we communicate our appreciation of anything else we grow or even life on the farm in general? Would we have understood any of this a year ago? No, not with any depth. If someone else had told us the same things, we would have said, "I'm happy for you, that's great," and moved on with the conversation. A year earlier, we didn't know what we didn't know. Now life without the farm just would not be the same.

I said, "Hold on. I've been reading those stories from Dad's chest. Let me get one. I want to read it to you." I retrieved the following story and read it for Brian and Kate.

> *I grew up with great cooks and great food at home. My mother was Italian and my father was Cajun. My mom cooked traditional Italian dishes that often had soffritto (carrots, onions, celery and some garlic) as a base. Dad cooked classic Cajun dishes with "The Holy Trinity" of Cajun cooking (onions, celery and bell peppers) as a base. The house always smelled so good around dinner time as the vegetables, herbs, meat, pasta and rice were cooking away.*

Food was always a topic of conversation and a reason for lots of activity in our house. My brother, sister and I learned from our parents how to cook several traditional dishes (Chicken Cacciatore, Spaghetti Bolognese, Crawfish Étouffée, Gumbo). By the time I was 13 I could cook entire dinners for the whole family. When I was about 16 I started experimenting with blending Italian and Cajun dishes. Some of my experiments were really good; others were not worth repeating. But, I loved - absolutely loved - to cook, and eat.

After college I got a job that involved living on multiple islands in The Kingdom of Tonga in the South Pacific for a year. It was a once-in-a-lifetime opportunity, so I was glad to accept the assignment. The trip there was long but the places and people were wonderful. I also enjoyed their traditional foods. I ate fish, banana, yams, taro and breadfruit. I enjoyed learning about traditional preparation methods. Several families invited me to their homes for meals, which were a wonderful celebration of life.

After a few months I really started missing some of the dishes I grew up on. So, I went to the local store to get the ingredients to make a gumbo or étouffée. While the items were more expensive than back in the US, they had everything I needed with one exception. Celery. They had no celery, at all. The shop keeper (and others I contacted on other Tongan islands) said there had been a blight of some kind at the farm where their supplier bought produce. It wiped out the celery crop. I asked what it would take to get some and I was told it could be obtained (as with anything else) for the right price. What that meant was finding someone somewhere with an airplane who would make a special trip to get celery, fly it to Tonga, etc. The bottom line was if it was worth $500 I could indeed get some celery. I decided I would manage without it.

I made my way back to my small apartment and began opening my packages, excited to taste something familiar, something that said "home" to me in a familiar way. I sautéed the bell peppers and onions, noting - sadly - that the third member of the Trinity was absent. I added in the shrimp, more seasoning, cooked a few minutes then added the flour. Oh yeah, it was coming together and looking good, but I had to admit that it lacked something in the aroma. "Oh well," I said, "It's gonna be good!" I finished preparing the dish and sat down to enjoy a big bowl of shrimp étouffée. I raised the first spoonful to my nose to take in the multi-faceted aroma of comfort itself. It was good. I brought the spoon to my mouth and let the savory blanket of flavor cascade over my tongue and all around my mouth. It was beautiful. The shrimp had just enough "snap" when I bit into them. The spices were all playing nicely together. However, I noticed the absence of a crunch and a unique taste sensation that made this good dish - different. Was it étouffée? Well, yes... but Daddy would not have said so. Mind you, I ate half the skillet that night and the other half the next day. I enjoyed it. It was good! But, it was different - not the same.

That celery blight deprived me of celery for a year. So, for a year my étouffée and bolognese I made for myself and for friends were good, but not the same as I grew up with. I found myself telling my dinner guests that the dishes were even better with celery, which they acknowledged politely. But, I could tell they didn't really get it. They didn't eat much celery anyway and they had never had étouffée or bolognese sauce in their lives, so they had no real frame of reference. They did not know what they were missing, but I did. They were grateful for "really good" food but I knew they could have had "awesome" food.

When my time in Tonga came to an end, I made my way back to the States. I had learned how to cook with taro and breadfruit as well as coconuts. I had shared my family's food culture (for the most part) with my Tongan friends.

When I landed back home I went to my apartment and dropped off my bags. The next thing I did was to make my way to the market and stock up on more affordable ingredients to make the dishes I missed just the way I like them. The market had bright green, leafy, beautiful celery in abundant supply. I bought two bunches. I went home. I made a bolognese and an étouffée to last me the whole week! Oh, when I ate dishes with those sauces, all was right once again. I had taken for granted the ever-present, simple green stalks of celery and what they contribute to my culinary heritage. As I ate my spaghetti bolognese that night I began thinking about what - and who - in my life I take for granted as if it or they will just always be there, and always accepting of my whims and wishes. Not so. Blights hit crops, diseases hit people. Life is precious and full of challenges. I should take nobody for granted. I got grateful for people and things that can be here today and gone tomorrow.

This has been a story about food. But when I lived it, it became a metaphor for life. It began a journey in my mind and my heart that has continued to this day. I started thinking and feeling more deeply about things, people and God. I felt thankful, grateful and I couldn't imagine being grateful to "the universe". No, gratitude had to be toward a person. Living gratefully has become a way of life.

Chapter 14: Library Talk

We had been living on the farm for a little over a year when Kate made a trip to the library in town. She had been to the library a few times in that first year, but she had not had extensive conversations with anyone there. She was checking out some books when the librarian asked her if she was related to my folks, because of our last name. Kate told her that I had inherited the farm and we had moved there and been running it for the last year or so. The librarian said of Dad, "You know, I was here for the first talk he gave. It had a profound impact on me. In fact, I still have the flyer I had picked up that promoted the talk. I keep it in my dresser drawer to remind me." Kate asked what "talk" she was referring to. The librarian said, "If you have a minute I will show you in our archives." They both walked over to a cabinet where the librarian found a particular folder and pulled out a flyer. There was Dad's name, the date and the time of his talk at the library. The mayor was listed as the emcee for the night. The topic? "Celery Day". Under that appeared "You will be glad you came."

Kate thanked the librarian for mentioning the event and showing her the flyer. She asked if she could get a photocopy of the flyer, which the librarian was glad to do. When Kate got home she said, "Mike, you won't believe what I just heard," and she told me what the librarian had shared with her. Then, she handed me the copy of that flyer. I sat on the couch with my mouth open and the photocopied flyer in my hand, with a clear sense that I knew only parts of the story and that was not going to be enough for me. I thought, "There has to be a connection between the stories in the chest and this talk at the library. The librarian even said it was his "first talk", so there were subsequent talks." I had to know the connection, the story that linked Dad and the library talk with those stories. I went to the chest and retrieved the "Celery Day" box. I had read many of the stories, but not all of them. So, I took all the stories - every sheet of paper - out of the box and began looking over them for anything Dad might have written about this talk at the library. I looked at each piece of paper in that box and found nothing that shed light on the talk or the origin of the stories. I tried to think through what the connection could be. Some of those stories were from out of state, even out of the country. What in the world would my dad have said at our local library, that had anything to do with celery, that people came to hear - not once, but more than once - that somehow caused people elsewhere in the state, elsewhere in the country and even elsewhere in the world to write their stories and send them to Dad? I thought, and walked around my study and talked my way through two cups of tea trying to connect these facts that were so clearly estranged from their context. I just couldn't see the thread that ran through them all. I finally decided to stop the quest for the night and just put everything back in the box and go to bed and try another day. As I lifted the lid off the box to replace the stories, I caught a glimpse of a shiny reflection inside the box, on the bottom. I moved the box more into the light of my lamp and tilted it back and forth. The reflection was from writing on the bottom of the box in pencil, and in Dad's handwriting. It read, "May 25th - Celery Day".

"What does that mean exactly?" I thought. I wondered why Dad wrote those words inside the box. Why write those words there? Why would you write those words without an explanation? Why wouldn't you write something more substantial, maybe in … your journal. The journal. I had taken Dad's journal out of the chest when we spent those exploratory three weeks at the farm and put it in the desk drawer in the study. I promptly pulled open the drawer and found the journal tucked into the back of the drawer. I loosened the leather strap that wound around the journal to keep it closed. As I opened the journal I could see that there was a folded sheet of paper between two pages of the journal, near the back. I turned to those pages where the folded sheet was kept. On the left hand page was an entry for May 25th from four years earlier. It read, "Today is my Celery Day. I will forever be grateful, every day. Sure, I will always work to improve, to grow, but I will be grateful along the way. I will be grateful to God for what I have and who I have in my life, every day. Always remember the prison lesson." The entries on the right hand page were not related to a talk at the library nor to the stories. So, I decided to see what was on the folded piece of paper. When I opened it, another piece of paper fell out. What fell out was a flyer for that first talk at the library. It was worn around the edges and there were names written on the back. The other sheet of paper, which was also worn around the edges, contained the following story.

Bang. Bang. Bang.

Bang. Bang. Bang.

It was that familiar staccato rapping of wood on metal... getting closer... louder... as always, announcing that it was time to get up according to Officer Daniels and the State. My eyes wanted to stay shut and just return to the dream I was having. But, not so. I knew it was time so I opened them and looked around, on the off chance that just maybe the dream had been real and prison was the dream. Hhhmmmm... hard bed, hard walls, stainless steel sink I can touch with my foot... stainless steel toilet right next to it. Either this was the biggest airplane restroom in history with a bed... or it was day 2,197 of a very real prison sentence.

That's when I heard the opening grunt and groan from above. Ah, Josh was beginning his morning in typical fashion: top shelf expletives accenting a familiar recitation of how much he hated being here, how he didn't deserve to be here, how the food stinks, the staff are morons, the laundry where he works is cruel and unusual punishment, those guys who ratted him out really should be in here instead of him, etc., etc, etc., etc., etc. I could have recited his pledge to another day of bitterness and self pity right along with him. No thanks.

I see the same stuff as Josh, and everyone else here. When I first made my "housing reservation" with the State via Judge Lippett's court, I hated everything and every one. I was like Josh, only worse. I nearly broke my foot kicking the cell door one night, like that was going to help. I was mad because life wasn't fair; I didn't deserve this… place. I didn't deserve the smells, the indignity of searches, the boredom, the 23 library books or the food. I sure didn't deserve to roll around in all this splendor by myself. No, there were two other guys who should have been in here instead of me. I was unlucky; not worse than those other two, just unlucky. I made my own pledge to another day of bitterness and self pity, and recited it with relentless consistency… every single morning.

One day on the yard I decided to talk to an old timer who was never going to breathe free air again. I figured either he would be a picture of ongoing rage against the injustice of being here, or he would look defeated, resigned to his fate… blank. I approached him and gave him my name, he gave me his. We swapped "What are you in for?" info and just as we finished it was time to go back in. We talked the next few times outside about this and that; nothing too heavy.

Then came the conversation I will never forget. We met out on the yard. He greeted me. I don't remember what I said next, but I will never forget what he said next. He said, "Son, you look like I looked a long time ago. Let me guess, life's not fair, you wish you could pound on somebody responsible for you being here and every day you feel like you are going to explode. Is that about right?" I said, "Yeah, pretty close old timer." He said,

"Since you started this discussion, let me tell you something important I've learned: You gotta get grateful, or you will live bitter and die bitter. I've been grateful for many years now and it has made a huge difference for me."

"Grateful?!? Grateful for what?!?" I thought. In fact, before I could catch myself, I blurted out those words. He nodded his head up and down. "Yeah, I know. Hard to be grateful when life ain't perfect, right?" he said. "Not perfect? That's and understatement old timer! Have you forgotten this hole we live in now?" I replied.

He smiled; just smiled. He looked at the ground for a bit… concrete next to hard packed dirt with a single weed poking up through a crack in the earth. He asked me, "You see this? What is it?" I said, "It's a weed. So what?" and crossed my arms and looked away, then back at him. He smiled again. He said, "You see a weed. I see the flowers on the green plant growing right here in front of me, in this place, in this dirt packed down by convict shoes for 100 years. You think the plant would choose this if it could? Probably not. But here it is, and it's alive and growing. It does what it was meant to do, even here. It gives me another thing to be grateful for."

I reluctantly saw what he was saying. I saw it with some stingy little piece of my brain and with a lot of internal resistance, but I saw it. I did not embrace it though. My anger, bitterness and frustration had become my identity. We don't surrender our identity lightly.

I looked him in the eye. I saw a flicker, a brightness that I still remember. I didn't know what to do with that, but it was there. I decided to act as if I had not seen it. "So, old timer" I said, "I need to get grateful, huh? Grateful to who? Momma? The warden? The judge? My former friends? God? Who?" He said, "Well, more than one of those really. But, if you don't get grateful to God, you *will never know him and never live in deep peace that nobody can take away from you."*

I wanted to respond, to laugh out loud, or yell at him, or make fun of him… but I just stood there and looked away. He was telling me to get grateful to God when nothing in my life had changed. He was telling me that he learned to be grateful to God while in this hole of a place. "Man, that's a tough pill to swallow. I have to think about that one," I said. He looked me in the eye, without a smile this time. It was a look that seemed to go through my eyes and down into my soul. I knew it was sincere concern… love, really… like a son always wants from his dad. He said, "I know it is. I'm not saying you need to sign up to think everything I think or believe everything I believe. I'm saying I know that we are designed by God to walk with him. I'm saying embrace a lifelong journey with God that starts with being grateful for being alive and asking him to show himself to you. He made himself known in a way we can understand when Jesus came and lived on earth. God put his will and his message to us in a person, in Jesus. I'm talking about a real person who I know and I walk with every day. I'm not talking about a bunch of religion or rituals and stuff. When I understood God wanted me, I started getting grateful. When I surrendered my life to Jesus, I got really grateful. I'm saying you can have this too." I said, "Well, that's a lot to take in too old timer. I'll think it over. Looks like we have to go in now. Hey, thanks for talking with me." He smiled and said, "I'm glad to know you. Think about what I said. It's true and real and yours if you want it." Then, we both walked back inside, lined up once again, back to the box, the smells, the food.

That was about six weeks ago. I only saw the old timer a few more times in the yard. He passed on shortly after that conversation I remember so well. But, his words, his eyes and the spirit in him stayed with me.

Well, I got grateful. I knew if I didn't, I'd either twist off or wither. I started by saying out loud I was grateful to be alive and went from there. It took awhile but in my journey of gratefulness I came to believe in Jesus, not in a casual way, but for real. Now, I'm grateful for a lot, and it has changed my life, even in this place where I live. I've got a little more than a year left to go. That's okay, I'll just keep being trained while I'm here.

You know, I just remembered, today is the day. A couple years back, the budget cuts meant our food had to get cheaper, which has meant a lot of beans and potatoes. Man, it's plain food, but I am grateful. But today, today is the day. I look forward to it every week and I'm thankful, grateful. Today I get something I've come to appreciate more than I ever did before. Today is celery day and I am thankful for the flavor it brings to my life.

I looked at the story, the journal entry and the flyer. I thought, "The story and flyer are in the journal at this specific page, no doubt for a reason. How would a story about two guys in prison connect to May 25th for Dad and how does his talk connect to either one? The talk was on July 15th, which was after that May 25th journal entry. Something happened May 25th and it made a big impact in Dad's life, then he talked about it at the library on July 15th using the same title as the journal entry. But, what about the prison story? The only prison connection I could think of was Dad's brother, my uncle Roy who was older than Dad and had been in prison a long, long time before he died there. Wait. Roy died four years ago, in June. The old timer in the story, was that Roy?

Chapter 15: Connection

The next morning I updated Kate and asked if she would try to talk to the librarian and get her recollection of the talk Dad had given. I decided to contact Mr. Umberger, who had been mayor at the time of that talk. I called his home and after introducing myself I asked if he remembered that talk. He said, "I sure do. I don't think I can forget it." I said, "Sir, I would like to sit down with you and hear your recollection of that talk. Could I buy you some coffee today or tomorrow?" He said, "Well, these days my schedule is remarkably free. How about 3pm at Edna's on main street?" I said, "I will see you there."

Kate and I each connected with the people we wanted to hear from. That evening Brian was out with Violet and some other friends and we were more interested in sharing what we learned than in making dinner. So, I brought home some great food and coconut cream pie from Edna's. We each got our food lined out on our plates and sat down quickly. Kate said, "The librarian's name is Linda. She said, "I remember how humble and straightforward he was when he spoke. He said he had met a young man who was in prison who shared a story about getting grateful, specifically for, well, celery. I know it sounds crazy! Who is thankful for celery, right? That story helped him with feeling stuck and kind of burned out on farming and not very thankful. I remember he said that was why the talk was titled "Celery Day". The point was getting grateful for who and what you have."

I then shared my findings with Kate. I said, "Mr. Umberger told me he remembered Dad telling how he had become kind of 'fussy' or dissatisfied with his lot in life. He had gotten older and couldn't work like he used to on the farm. He had to hire more help. He wasn't getting the prices he thought he should for his produce. Then he visited someone close to him - an older man - who was in prison.

He said in the course of that conversation the old man told him there had been a change at the prison that meant something to him, that he was thankful for. He said, "Ha, I remember everyone sitting on the edge of their seats at that point. Your dad had really built the moment up for everyone. The air was thick with anticipation. Then he said the old man told him, 'A couple of months ago they gave us celery to eat at lunch time. I hadn't even seen a fresh vegetable in a long time. I hadn't had celery for years. I'm telling you, it was nice to taste something so fresh and flavorful. I know folks on the outside don't think it's a big deal but to me it is. Hey, they say we will probably get celery every Thursday, at least as long as the money lasts to buy it. I was so happy, I declared that day 'Celery Day'. I put it on my wall, off where you can't see it easily. That note reminds me there is more in the world and more to life than what I see and feel in my little box. And, I am thankful for life every day, even the so-called little things.' Mike, I've never forgotten that talk. In fact, I asked your dad if he would share that same talk again at the library. He agreed and gave that talk a few more times at the library and I think he even shared it in Tulsa a couple of times and at a couple of prisons in the state, and probably elsewhere." Kate and I both looked at each other. We now knew what had happened with Dad.

He had been going to see his brother Roy in prison for years. One day Roy (the old timer) shared his "Celery Day" story with Dad. Dad realized he had nothing to complain about and plenty to be thankful for, especially since Roy had become grateful for a vegetable, and one most people take for granted. Dad made the May 25th journal entry his stake in the ground to say, "I will be grateful to God for what I have and who I have in my life, every day." I had heard him say that before but I didn't realize where the saying came from.

But, what about the story from the younger guy in prison? Where did that come from? I remembered Dad and I talking after uncle Roy died. He said to me, "Roy had some rough experiences with religion early in life. Unfortunately he "threw the baby out with the bathwater" and had nothing to do with not only religion but with God for a long time. His choices landed him in prison and that's where he opened his heart to the Lord - not to dead religion - but to the reality he had been running from, or didn't know was really there. In his last years he sought to be salt and light to the men in prison. He told me in the last few months of his life that he thought a young man who he had been talking to was seeing some light, some hope. I'm going to visit that young man if he will see me." So, Dad must have gone to visit that young man after Roy passed away. Then, the young man wrote down his story and sent it to Dad.

I didn't know how to find the young man who had written the prison story because he didn't sign the story or use his name in it. Maybe he didn't want his name attached to prison for future reference. I did remember that there were names on the back of that flyer from the first talk. As I researched those names, I found most of the folks still lived in the county. As I contacted them, I asked if they remembered the talk and if they brought anyone with them to the first talk, or to the other talks Dad gave. Many had gone to the first talk and to other talks, and had taken friends or relatives with them. One lady had taken some relatives to hear one of Dad's talks around Christmas time. She had a nephew who was staying at her house for a few days who went to the talk with her. It turns out, he worked for a certain national magazine that deals with geographic stories, and the people who live in those geographies. After the talk and the holiday he went on assignment - to Mongolia. After that? To east Africa, specifically Malawi.

I thanked her for the phone conversation and hung up. I had to sit still for awhile to let this sink in. This nephew of hers had come back to Okfuskee county for the Christmas holiday with his family, heard Dad's talk and apparently took the message with him overseas. I don't know if he looked for opportunities to share the message with people, or if their genuine gratitude for celery triggered his memory. In either case, there is no doubt he played a key role in "the goat brothers" and Sarangerel sharing their stories in writing, ultimately with Dad and eventually with me.

Emotions flooded my heart and mind at that point. I wept when I realized the reach of a simple story of thankfulness, all the way from a prison in Oklahoma to a young lady in Mongolia. I realized that these other stories from the chest must all have some connection back to the talks, either at the library down the road from our farm, a prison in the state or elsewhere. The essence of that story may have been transmitted to 3 or 4 or 10 connections out from those folks at the talk. Some of these stories may have come from a lady whose mom was a friend of a cousin of a co-worker of an old schoolmate of a... you get the point. The vital, core essence of the story has power, and that power is transferrable. That power taps into a core spiritual discipline that I had struggled with - being grateful, thankful.

One guy I called said that a friend of his son's was probably the guy who set up the computer lab in the impoverished part of the city. He said that guy (Gabe) was a professor at a university now and gave me his number. I called Gabe and he said that was him. He remembered writing the story and sending it to Dad.

Dad entrusted that chest, with those stories, to me... counting on me to be thankful enough for my family to take the time to look in that chest. What if I had just ignored the chest and said, "You know, let's just sell the farm. Let's just sell the whole thing - furniture and all - as is. We have lives already, etc, etc." He counted on me to see the "Future Crop Plan" envelope. He counted on me to figure out the connection between the stories and the talks. I thought, "Man, that seems like a big risk to take Dad. Why didn't you just tell me all this? If I hadn't read what was in the chest and cared to understand it, all that would have been lost. I don't get it."

A couple of days later, I was having my morning tea, and I was wondering again why Dad left such a valuable story to me to find. We had talked several times in the weeks before he passed away and he never mentioned anything about the stories. I began to wonder if he had journaled about the stories, the talks, etc. I retrieved Dad's journal and thumbed through the last several pages. On the last two pages I read the following:

> *"Mike, if you discover the box and the stories you may wonder why I never shared it with you. I did share about being grateful, but not the "Celery Day" thing. Candidly, I was not sure you would see it for what it is, and might disregard it as an off-the-wall idea. It was not and is not. It's a symbol for being thankful and it means a great deal to me.*
>
> *Even if you never see this journal or the box of stories, the story Roy shared with me May 25th and the message of living gratefully is out there circulating among people. It has affected many lives positively already and I think it will continue to do so as it is shared.*
>
> *I learned from Roy's story that he told me face-to-face, from the young man in prison who wrote the first story I ever received and I learned from all the*

other stories that were sent to me. I have learned to be grateful for:

> **DI**scovery - of new people and things
> **G**rowth - development and expansion of what is precious
> **MO**tivation - to stop taking people or things for granted
> **RE**covery - of the value of people and things

I condensed what I've learned about living gratefully to the following which is easy to remember: Live Gratefully, Eat Celery, DIG MORE.

By the way son, I knew that if you didn't look into the chest on your own, Kate or Brian would. One way or another, what I've learned about living gratefully was going to get to your family. I know the three of you too well to think otherwise.

If you do "get it" - really get it - then you know what to do. If you don't get it, please ask Kate if she does.   - Much love, Dad"

I had to smile when I read the last couple of lines. Dad was telling me - only half jokingly - that if I had missed the point, I should involve Kate to facilitate my understanding. That was always good advice anyway, so I had to agree. I felt like I did "get it" regarding the "Celery Day" concept and its impact on Dad's life. He put it to practice when he realized he had taken the farm and his career as a farmer for granted. He got truly grateful for the farm and his career and began to value both in a deep, thoughtful way that affected his behavior. Out of that the farm began to grow and develop. He discovered new plants to grow and harvest, and new means of doing so. He had to put the concept to practice in being grateful for Mom's remaining days when she got sick. He finished out his days on earth visiting people and having folks visit him, sharing stories, laughing, underscoring the ideas and commitments that make life deeply meaningful.

I shared that last journal entry with Kate and Brian the next day. Kate said she felt like she had discovered farm life and seen growth in our lives as farmers, because of being grateful for the opportunity we had to pursue this new lifestyle. Brian felt the same about the farm, and about Violet. She had understandably been the top discovery of the last several months for Brian. He was grateful for his relationship with Violet and was nurturing and developing it accordingly. I said I had become more grateful for my parents, for uncle Roy, for the farm and for Kate and Brian than ever.

After dinner, I went for a walk by myself. I made my way to where the varieties of celery were growing, away from any other human eyes or ears. I found a place in the patch and knelt down on the earth. I felt my knees sink into the soil, the same soil that four generations of my family had worked and that I now work. The sense of connection I felt - to my ancestors, to the land, to my wife and son, to our fellow farm workers, to our customers - was overwhelming. I looked toward the sky, with tears streaming down my face and smiled. I said, "Dad, I do get it, I really do. Thank you for all you have shared with me - the ideas, the heart, the farm… everything. I love you Dad." I raised my hands to the sky and said, "Thank you Lord for my life - for the people, places and things that matter most. I get it - living gratefully is something you designed us all for. It's good for us. It's essential to having a relationship with you. While I'm grateful for a lot, I'm saying now that I am particularly grateful for our family farm, something I had not valued much for many years. I have recovered the value of this place. And right here in this celery patch I declare today - September 8th - is my Celery Day." I stayed there for several minutes just soaking in the value of making that declaration that this day was now a permanent marker for me, a reminder for the rest of my life to live gratefully - always. I walked back to the house, hugged my wife and son and had the best night's sleep I have had in years.

The following week Kate, Brian and I started working on what we knew needed to be done. We needed to continue sharing what Dad and folks from all over had learned. We knew a lot of people, old and young, rich and poor, city and rural folks, of every race and nationality, who would benefit from the story that started it all - a prisoner who was grateful for a "small thing" like celery. The stories in the box so far all had an actual connection to celery, which was great. But, the core truth of living gratefully was always the main thing, whether someone ever ate celery or not. As we share with others, hopefully, they will embrace that core truth and have their own "Celery Day", and maybe even send their story to us. Just imagine where all this could go.

ABOUT THE AUTHOR

Steve is a regular guy who loves his wife and children and is thankful for his friends. He sees life as a God-given journey, including things we can overlook. He wants to give and receive wisdom and strength through interacting with others, to make life count as much as possible.

ONGOING CONNECTIONS

"Celery Day" is all about being grateful as we move through our journey on earth. Of all we can be grateful for, the people in our lives matter most.

I would welcome the opportunity to connect with you and others who want to share words of substance that bring life, light and hope to each other.

My Facebook page: facebook.com/SteveQueenWords

Facebook group: Celery Day - Discussion for Readers of the Book

Twitter: @SteveQueenWords

THE FOLLOWING PAGES ARE A PLACE TO STORE YOUR HARVEST FROM "CELERY DAY".

WHAT CAN YOU GLEAN FROM MIKE?

WHAT CAN YOU GLEAN FROM KATE?

WHAT CAN YOU GLEAN FROM BRIAN?

WHAT CAN YOU GLEAN FROM MIKE'S DAD?

WHICH OF THE STORIES FROM THE CHEST WAS
YOUR FAVORITE?
WHAT CAN YOU GLEAN FROM THAT STORY?

WHICH OF THE STORIES FROM THE CHEST WAS
YOUR SECOND FAVORITE?
WHAT CAN YOU GLEAN FROM THAT STORY?

DO YOU HAVE "CELERY DAYS" IN YOUR LIFE, WHEN YOU GOT REALLY GRATEFUL FOR SOMEONE OR SOMETHING?

HAVE YOU "PUT A STAKE IN THE GROUND" TO KEEP THOSE MOMENTS OF CLARITY IN YOUR HEART AND MIND? HOW?

Please feel free to share you comments and stories on the Facebook group.

Made in the USA
Charleston, SC
23 December 2014